Communications
in Computer and Information Science   **1067**

Commenced Publication in 2007
Founding and Former Series Editors:
Phoebe Chen, Alfredo Cuzzocrea, Xiaoyong Du, Orhun Kara, Ting Liu,
Krishna M. Sivalingam, Dominik Ślęzak, Takashi Washio, and Xiaokang Yang

Editorial Board Members

More information about this series at http://www.springer.com/series/7899

Anjum Naweed · Lorelle Bowditch ·
Cyle Sprick (Eds.)

Intersections
in Simulation and Gaming

Disruption and Balance

Third Australasian Simulation Congress, ASC 2019
Gold Coast, Australia, September 2–5, 2019
Proceedings

 Springer

Editors
Anjum Naweed (iD)
Appleton Institute for Behavioural Science
Central Queensland University
Wayville, SA, Australia

Lorelle Bowditch
Appleton Institute for Behavioural Science
Central Queensland University
Wayville, Australia

Cyle Sprick
College of Medicine and Public Health
Flinders University
Adelaide, Australia

ISSN 1865-0929   ISSN 1865-0937 (electronic)
Communications in Computer and Information Science
ISBN 978-981-32-9581-0   ISBN 978-981-32-9582-7 (eBook)
https://doi.org/10.1007/978-981-32-9582-7

This Springer imprint is published by the registered company Springer Nature Singapore Pte Ltd.
The registered company address is: 152 Beach Road, #21-01/04 Gateway East, Singapore 189721, Singapore

Preface

What am I?
> I can be *swung* and *hung*.
> I can be *thrown off*.
> I can be *tipped* and *tilted*.
> I can be *struck*.
> I am frequently associated with *power*.
> I am often linked with *checks*.
> The answer of course is: *Balance!*

Welcome to Intersections in Simulation and Gaming: Disruption and Balance, an intimate compilation of research presented at the 2019 Australasian Simulation Congress (ASC 2019). Held in the Gold Coast and under the auspices of Simulation Australasia, this volume contains peer-reviewed papers selected from the proceedings of the 23rd Simulation Technology and Training conference, the 14th Simulation Health conference, and the 8th Serious Games Showcase and Challenge—Australia. But what is the link with "Balance" we hear you asking. Well, there are several, allow us to expand.

Today, there is a near-constant stream of commentary within news and media about the increasing rate of advancements in technology, and the consequential impact this has upon our lives. Automation and artificial intelligence are taking over human jobs, even as they ever-optimize how we work and create efficiencies. Worry about a loss of privacy abounds, as do concerns for cyber security in our ever-growing number of connected devices. But it is not only technology that has a role in all this. Our interactions with one another have evolved along with our expectations. Life and our place within it seem suddenly so very disrupted and out of balance. For this reason, we conceptualized the congress around themes of dualism, and the notion of disruption and balance.

In many ways, balance and disruption are contrary and seemingly opposite forces, but they have an intriguing relationship. Is it possible, for example, to strike a balance through disruption, or for disruption to be an agent of balance? The ASC 2019 represented an opportunity to consider how simulation and its interstices with technology, training, health, and serious games, may help achieve a balance between the conflicting priorities of today's needs vs preparing us for the disruption of an uncertain future. Now more than ever, we need to strike a balance with the lure of new technologies applicable to simulation by ensuring that they are being applied in a considered way, and leading to results that are valid, whether they be for teaching and training, decision making or other domains.

Although the papers in this book have broadly overlapping topics, they have very different dimensions, thus in structuring this book, we considered how the disruption and/or balance was observed, effected or framed according to the essences of each paper.

In the first section of the book, disruption and balance as the theory underpinning some very human dimensions in simulation is explored; we examine this first by focusing systematically and multifacetedly on the facilitation of simulation, where balance is often approached through intended though uncertain disruption, and then through individual situation awareness in a simulated reconnaissance task.

In the second section of the book, we turn our approach to gaming experience, first through avatar creation and connectivism in clinical practice, and then by understanding how gamers cope with disruptive external stressors in internet gaming.

In the third section of the book, we venture into the design and application of simulation, first by disrupting the debate raging between theory and practice in design of learning, and then by investigating balance between technology-driven design of experience and successful outcomes.

In the fourth section of the book, we move squarely to modeling and simulation for search and rescue to examine questions of balance in the number of agents in a swarm, and also in the emergent behaviors of these unmanned autonomous assets.

The fifth and final section of the book approaches balance in technology and training within the defense-sector, initially between technical skills and service experience, and then through machine learning and physiological metrics.

While modest in number, the selection of peer-reviewed papers in this book illustrate the variety of topics discussed over three days of scientific presentations, workshops, and keynote addresses in the program. The review process was double-blind with qualifying papers allocated three reviewers to ensure a well-based editorial decision. Key criteria for reviewer feedback and acceptance included the scope of the paper, the scientific and technical quality of the work, any innovations used in methods, findings and/or applications, potential for impact, and clarity of presentation.

The papers defining this volume capture balance and disruption on emerging trends and display creativity, versatility, and innovation in their approaches. In this book, we also have the pleasure of welcoming the first ever full-length papers for Simulation Health, a conference that has traditionally involved long abstracts. It is a privilege to be able to bring this work to you.

The editors wish to thank all of the authors for their work and the many reviewers who took the time out to consider their research and provide feedback. We also gratefully acknowledge the outstanding work of everyone listed in the Organization pages in helping to bring the conference together.

September 2019
Anjum Naweed
Lorelle Bowditch
Cyle Sprick

Organization

Conference Convener

Philip Swadling   Thales, Australia

Conference Stream Conveners

Sharon Clipperton   Mater Education, Australia
Fred Hardtke   Raytheon, Australia
Dale Linegar   Oztron Media, Australia

Scientific Conveners

Anjum Naweed   Central Queensland University, Australia
Cyle Sprick   Flinders University, Australia

Scientific Co-convener

Lorelle Bowditch   Central Queensland University, Australia

2019 ASC Program Committee

Liz McNeill   Flinders University, Australia
John Paige   Louisiana State University, USA
Janiece Roche   Simulation Australasia Ltd., Australia
Ryan Stephenson   Bohemia Interactive Simulations, Australia
Jessica Stokes-Parish   Simulation Australasia Ltd., Australia

Contents

Defence-Oriented Technology and Training

Human Dimensions

Focusing the 'Gaze' on Facilitators of Simulation

Elyssebeth Leigh[1]([✉]) and Anjum Naweed[2]([✉]) [iD]

[1] FutureSearch, Sydney, NSW 2044, Australia
elyssebeth.leigh@icloud.com
[2] Appleton Institute of Behavioural Science, Central Queensland University,
Wayville, SA 5034, Australia
anjum.naweed@cqu.edu.au

Abstract. Much of the literature on the concept of simulation as a "safe container" is focused on creating safety for participants. However, recent research is starting to bring to light the vulnerabilities within the persons facilitating simulations. Facilitators operate in many different simulator contexts, each of which shapes their behaviours and in turn influences any specific concerns they may have for their simulation participants. Given the paucity of research in this area, this paper takes the approach of examining the facilitator from four different perspectives. The first concept is that of 'novice to expert' (Benner 1984) to help frame aspects of the learning curve commonly experienced by simulation facilitators. The second is that of the power relationships in operation throughout the life of a simulation. The third concept concerns the phenomenology of body memory (Fuchs 2012) and its potential to unexpectedly intrude on events. The fourth is the sociological concept of 'the gaze,' highlighting the social dynamics of control and the impact of the awareness of the self in context and in the act of seeing and being seen in operation in simulated contexts. Taken together, these concepts influence and shape facilitator performance and behaviour both consciously and unconsciously. In contrast to literature on the related concept of simulation as a safe container for promoting the safety of participants, the facilitator is conceptualised as a system actor also in need of attention to ensure they are well prepared, feel safe themselves and have access to robust backup systems and tools that provide relevant and timely guidelines for action. This paper examines each concept in turn, making links among them explicit, and exploring their role in the process of developing simulation specific facilitation skills.

Keywords: Simulation · Facilitator · Training · Safety

1 Introduction

Facilitators of simulations operate in many different contexts, each of which shapes their behaviours and influences their specific concerns in regard to each new process and the participants. While much attention is paid—in practice and in theory—to ensuring the design of the simulation is both a valid and verifiable replication of its real-world context, far less attention is paid to the skills required of the persons who are

A. Naweed et al. (Eds.): ASC 2019, CCIS 1067, pp. 3–12, 2019.
https://doi.org/10.1007/978-981-32-9582-7_1

tasked with ensuring the process operates as intended. In specific contexts, this role is variously called umpire, facilitator, manager or educator. This paper uses the term *'facilitator'* to cover all the variants for naming the role, as we examine it using four different perspectives. The first perspective is the concept known and understood as 'novice to expert' (Benner 1984) which helps to identify a learning curve traversed by anyone taking up the role. The second perspective is the complexity of managing the power relationships operating throughout (and sometimes beyond) the life of a simulation. The third perspective concerns awareness of issues related to the phenomenology of body memory (Fuchs 2012) and the potential for these to unexpectedly intrude upon and disturb events. The fourth and final perspective, to be considered in relation to each of these, is the sociological concept of 'the gaze,' which refers to the impact created by the fact of seeing and being seen. All four are vital, but usually hidden, factors influencing the degree of success in managing simulation-based learning contexts.

Together, these concepts directly influence and shape facilitator performance and behaviour both consciously and unconsciously, and this—in turn—shape and influence everything else that happens. This is considered in relation to the inter-connected variables of technical complexity and degree of fidelity in specific contexts. While the design of the simulation itself is often seen as the key causal factor in the success (or otherwise) of learning events and outcomes, this paper suggests that the skills of the facilitator are just as important, and at times, may even be the key determining factor for the achievement of learning goals.

2 Creating the Learning Context to be Managed

In order to 'come to life,' simulations need to be designed as accurate replicants of contexts and conditions relevant to specified learning goals. Further, they need to be managed in a manner that ensures they are valid and verifiable learning containers within which participants may explore knowledge and practice skills relevant to those goals. To achieve this, participants step into a 'role' in which they may find themselves doing something different—in some cases highly unusual—from their normal routines. Whatever the case, there is a tacit or implicit agreement for them to 'not be themselves' for the duration of the action in the simulation. However, facilitators are also 'in role' in a very particular way; the task required of their role is to hold the bounds of the whole experience stable, effectively providing a tangible albeit invisible 'container'. This can be thought of as a kind of 'shield' that allows participants to suspend their disbelief (S T Coleridge, quoted in Safire 2007) as learning emerges to match with individual needs and the simulation designer's intentions.

Simulations designed as learning contexts often have the capacity to unsettle (even disturb) participants along the way to acquiring new knowledge. Thus they can be—or become—'transformative' learning experiences (Mezirow 1991) as participants work to make meaning from unexpected and unanticipated events and their own, and others' responses. It is the facilitator's task to manage the container and its 'contents' in such a way that any nascent unease remains relative to the experience and eventually becomes a positive contribution to the learning process. While familiar with the particular design and its parameters in a way that participants are not, the facilitator must maintain a neutral demeanour to avoid giving positive or negative cues about behaviours they are observing. They must also ensure a sufficient degree of safety for everyone—including themselves, engendering the view that the container must be a 'safe container' (Rudolph et al. 2014). Thus, the quality of a learning environment is essentially the responsibility of the facilitator, who can create magic from a mediocre design, or limit the potential of a great one.

3 Four Perspectives for Exploring the Facilitator in the Context of 'Being in Role'

To examine how experienced facilitators are able to create both dissonance and sufficient safety in simulations, we examine the person in the role through four perspectives, respectively: (1) the progression of facilitators from novices to public acknowledgement of them as experts in the role; (2) the nature of the power relationships—both visible and unseen—that may need to be managed during the process; (3) the phenomenology of 'body memory' and how this may affect the flow of the action; and (4) the concept of the 'gaze' as a means of considering who is doing the looking, what is being looked at, and what the impact of this looking is[1].

3.1 From Novice to Expert

Facilitation of simulation can be done by anyone; for example, an expert clinician may take the role in a health simulation, or an expert tactician/strategist may manage a military simulation. While being acknowledged experts in their professional capacity, such individuals however are (and remain) novices in the role unless (and until) they devote attention to the task of learning the requirements of the role and rehearsing these in preparation for future activity as a facilitator. As described by Benner (1984), some individuals may find themselves on a trajectory from 'novice to expert,' drawn by the goal of improving their management of simulation-based learning.

Benner's framing of the novice-expert trajectory was developed from observation of nurses in training and such a conceptualisation is particularly useful here, as it illustrates that individuals can be both 'expert' and 'novice' depending on the context and its requirements. While a clinician or tactician has relevant expertise in their professional field, they may simultaneously lack an understanding of the requirements for managing learning in a simulated context and are thus novices in this domain.

Figure 1 is a representation of Benner's conception of the stages of skill acquisition from novice to expert. Nursing students have to move through the various stages shown in Fig. 1 and accept that much of their education will focus on actions required to complete the journey. On the contrary, facilitators of simulation-based learning, those who employ them, and those who design the tools they use, are often much less aware

---

[1] The authors are aware that they themselves have applied a form of 'the gaze' in this construction of paper by 'looking' directly at the facilitator role and its enactment.

of the scope of the learning involved in becoming 'expert' in the role. Currently, there are few available resources for acquiring expertise beyond repeated experiences in the role, and focused attention on using deep reflection and critical self-analysis, such as that called 'autobiographical awareness' by Torbert and Fisher (1992 p. 186) in their exploration of the practices of expert managers. While the International Association of Facilitators (2019) has a publicly available set of competencies for facilitators, these do not readily apply to the special circumstances in simulations which, by their very nature are designed to 'trick' human senses and perceptions in some specific way in order to replicate contexts that cannot otherwise be accessed for learning. Importantly, this 'trickery' places emphasis on a central feature of simulation as something that can be unsettling for individuals who prefer stability and order (Gilbert and Wilson 2009; Radonyi and Leigh 2016).

Stages of Skill Acquisition from Novice to Expert

Skill Level	Context	Perspective	Decision Making	Engagement
Novice	None	None	Analytical	None
Advanced Beginner	Situational	None	Analytical	None
Competent	Situational	Chosen	Analytical	Engaged Outcome
Proficient	Situational	Intuitive	Analytical	Engaged Goal, Outcome
Expert	Situational	Intuitive	Intuitive	Engaged Goal, Action, Outcome

Fig. 1. A systems representation of progressive development of skills (Eliason 2019)

The journey from novice to expert can be a lonely and complex one for a facilitator (Leigh 2003a; Thomas 2007), and the skills levels shown in Fig. 1 may not become evident until long after they are achieved. It is useful to note that intuition is considered a mark of expertise (Salas et al. 2010), implying as this does that the capability may not be evident to the persons possessing it, while being clearly visible to others observing the individual in action. For development of expertise as a facilitator, some factors are arguably necessary. These include: building mental models through repeated observation of behaviours in simulations, achieving a deep knowledge of patterns of human behaviour (Leigh 2003b); self-analysis; openness to external critique; capacity to accept (and learn from) failures; and a sense that learning must include a quotient of fun and the effort is worthwhile if it contributes to becoming a better manager of the next simulation.

3.2 Managing Power Relationships in a Simulation

The concept of managing power relationships in a simulation evokes a series of important questions. What is meant by 'power' and 'power relationships' in the context of simulations for learning? How do those who are involved in it perceive it? How do different individuals use it? What might constitute an 'abuse of power', and how does power as a construct relate to the way that simulations may apply forms of deception to replicate reality?

Designers of simulations create tools which invite participants to engage with 'unreal contexts' for the purpose of learning about some aspect of reality. The facilitator must use their twin-powers (of role and persuasion) to coax participants into believing the simulation is real enough for the purpose of nominated goals. Concepts of power are linked to a sense of psychological safety since feeling unsafe is directly linked to perceptions of losing power and control over self and context (Edmondson 2002). The task of creating unsettling environments to guide individuals towards new learning, invariably falls to the facilitator. This means that power—including how to identify and reframe personal parameters of psychological safety, and then how to work within or escape from contexts identified as unsafe—is always going to be contested to some degree within a simulation. Other issues related to concepts of power relationships within a simulation include ensuring that participants continue to feel powerful enough to sustain or maintain their own sense of identity while also becoming more able to question that identity, especially if/when this is part of the intended goals/outcomes for a particular use of a simulation.

The forgoing issues make managing power a challenging aspect of the facilitator's work. When the people and materials are assembled for a simulation, facilitators are usually the only persons present who know anything about what might happen next. This provides them with more power than that held by those in conventional teaching roles. In conventional 'teaching', repetition and familiarity convey to everyone what to expect from such contexts in which a designated person speaks and everybody else listens. Since, at the moment of entry into a simulation, only facilitators know what is intended, they have power of 'prior knowledge,' and considerable role-based power accorded to them because they are in charge of the ensuing activity. They also have skill and knowledge-based power in regard to how they frame the purpose, intentions, and learning processes.

Power Ratio and Foci through the Briefing, Action, and Debriefing Phases.
Simulations pass through three phases with power ratio and foci differing in each one.

Briefing. In the "briefing" phase, the facilitator prepares participants for a handover of power. Their actions and choices will go on to create a learning context framed by the designer's intentions. At this point, the focus on power is concentrated upon the tasks required to set the scene, the handing over of responsibility to participants, and ensuring an effective transition from passive to active learning engagement.

Action. Throughout the second *"action"* phase, participants must act and interact without interference from the facilitator, whose stance must be that of observer-coach who cannot step into the action (except under very specific circumstances, which they must try to ensure do not arise). The importance of this handoff of power, cannot be overstated. The simulation has been designed to provide learners with the authority, space and equipment to create their own learning. This can be a troubling concept for learners used to (or more conformable with) being passive recipients of information. Familiar props and configurations (e.g. seats in straight lines facing the front of the room) are absent and there may appear to be no guidelines for how to act. Transitioning to 'doing' from 'listening' may not be easy, and while participants do have all the power, their unsettling concerns may be numerous: they may not know how to exercise power/take action, there may be an internalised fear that doing anything may cause an individual to appear foolish, and actions that seem to be uninformed may lead to 'failure' in some way that they can intuit but not name. An expert facilitator provides non-directive encouragement and support, to guide but not direct individuals, and the whole group through these strong albeit unexpressed, concerns.

Novice facilitators used to relying on professional expertise to direct learning, may inadvertently misuse this essential non-exercise of power if they begin to feel uncertain in their role. To *save face*, they may shift to solving and telling, only to have participants retaliate later by using their residual power from the action phase to assign blame to the facilitator for uncertain or negative outcomes saying, "*but you told me/us to do...*". During this phase, almost all of the power is exercised by participants. Who have (but may not be aware of) a good deal of personal power: to direct and maintain control of their own responses to context and events; to question events as they unfold; to accept (or reject) conditions of uncertainty; to reserve judgment until the end, or impose it early on. This is hard to map in advance - since participants do not have to reveal anything about their approach to/uses of power in real time.

In effect there is a great deal of 'potential power' available for use in a simulation. A key factor from the facilitator's perspective is that power ratios are unseen and possibly unstable, and if things go wrong it is more likely to be the facilitator whose power—and use of it—is likely to be questioned.

Debriefing. Finally, a redistribution and balancing of power occurs during the third "debriefing" phase, when both facilitator(s) and participants combine their observations and experiences to draw out the learning that each/all have encountered. Here, power resides in the facilitator's capacity to help everyone explore the totality of 'what just happened' and equally, in participants' willingness and capacity to express opinions, explore uncertainties, and identify new awareness and understanding. The balance should be equitably shared between participants and facilitator as the debriefing draws out the key elements and learning points from each particular iteration of a simulation. Uses of the word 'should' indicates that ratios can veer widely depending on a facilitator's perspective on how to draw out learning outcomes.

Power relationships in simulations are connected to the concept of 'open' and 'closed' games. First presented by Christopher and Smith (1987), this defines simulation designs as *puzzles* (closed activities where there is a known solution towards which participants are directed) or *problems* (open activities for which no prior solution is assigned and where participants' solutions are all equally acceptable). Research has shown how apparently 'closed' activities (e.g., 'Dot in a Circle,' (Scannell 1980 p. 237) can become 'open' when actions and reactions allow for alternative outcomes in unexpected conditions.

3.3　Managing the Phenomenology of Body Memory

The word 'memory' is generally considered to refer to mind-based recall of events, but there is more to memory than an objective 'recall at a distance.' As Fuchs notes (2012), memory *'comprises not only one's explicit recollections of the past, but also the acquired dispositions, skills, and habits that implicitly influence one's present experience and behavior'* (p. 9). This effectively suggests that anyone entering a simulation designed to generate any level of dissonance (for the purpose of acquiring new knowledge and skills), cannot predict exactly how they will behave in response to unfolding events. All human beings collect 'memories' that are then stored throughout the body in emotional, psychological and physical ways, and at some future time, may or may not be recalled or observed in action. Consider, for example, how a footballer can coordinate muscle, tactical thinking and hand-eye coordination (to name just three factors in play) and then one day execute a spectacular kick which triggers 'debate about broader social issues' (McIver 2019).

Since all human beings collect and store memories, whether for future use or simply as part of living, simulation facilitators require the awareness that (sometimes) the events generated by a simulation may trigger unexpected responses from some participants. However, it can be impossible to know in advance exactly which events might trigger what kinds of responses, so the best they can do is to prepare for the unexpected and act 'as if' all is normal—until it is not so. For example, there is an anecdote (source no longer available) from the 1960's, concerning a team of educators who were conducting a 'relaxation exercise' for a group of managers attending a corporate learning program. As participants lay on the floor following instructions to *'relax your toes, tighten them; relax your legs, tighten the muscles'* one participant began to scream and flail about. Everything came to an instant halt as he was taken aside and given time to calm down and regain equilibrium. It transpired that some 15 years prior, he had been blown out of an aircraft shot down during WW2. Without a parachute he was falling to certain death, and the relaxation exercise had brought back the physical sensation (memory) of falling through space knowing there was no safe landing ahead. As he was present in the room, it was clear he had survived; landing through trees into deep snow had broken bones but brought an unexpected reprieve. He did not know his body held that memory, nor could the educators have known. They had to respond to both his needs *in situ*, as well as those of the others present, who were affected by his reactions but unaware of what had caused them.

Learning to respond mindfully to such totally unpredictable moments is an essential aspect of a facilitator's learning regime. The uniqueness of human experiences makes it impossible to anticipate all contingencies while the need to be prepared is clearly central to becoming an effective facilitator of a simulation as a 'safe container' for learning (Rudolph et al. 2014). Facilitators and participants are often aware of the potential for 'danger' when entering a simulation and as different simulation regimes prepare differently (Carrera et al. 2018), there is no one single formula for managing the content in preparation for unexpected events, that will be applicable to all contexts.

Work on the place of ethics in knowingly taking participants into unknown conditions is also being undertaken. Heeswijk (2018 unpublished) develops the argument that 'a facilitator of simulations and games needs to be both an ethical person and also pay close attention to the ethical conditions and issues as they *emerge* in those contexts [which is made both necessary and difficult by] complexity and social systems factors'.

Ethical behaviour and physiological 'memory' are interconnected and yet invisible components of a simulation, until some moment or action generates responses that do become visible. Expert facilitators are aware of the potential for such moments and, having spent time preparing themselves, are (usually) able to direct attention and action towards achieving acceptable results. Novice facilitators, being as yet unattuned to such eventualities, may feel a strong need to 'take over' in order to regain power and control of the simulation and of their own sense of unease. It is the very unexpectedness of the phenomenology of body memory that can most unsettle a novice facilitator while being absorbed into a framework for action by an expert.

3.4   Using—and Being Subject to—the 'Gaze'

The sociological concept of 'the gaze' (Chandler 2014) draws attention to the human state of awareness of being observed: being 'seen' and 'seeing' others. Its particular importance in the context of simulation is that 'being seen' can strongly influence facilitators in regard to how they perform in the role, subject as they are, to impact of 'the gaze' in at least two ways. First, there is the outward gaze of others while in role and managing specific activities, and then there is the reflected 'gaze' of themselves as they progress through phases of their own capability development from novice to expert.

Participants are unlikely to know the facilitator's own current assessment of their status in the role but would regard them as sufficiently expert to manage the process they anticipate experiencing. Although it may appear that 'gaze' is merely referring to looking and being looked at, '*it signifies a psychological relationship of power, in which the gazer is superior to the object of the gaze*' (Schroeder quoted in Chandler 2014). Regardless of matters of superiority in regard to relationships between 'observer' and 'observed,' it is the matter of awareness that focuses a facilitator's attention and can also influence participants. Awareness, or lack thereof, of the impact of being observed, can promote or seriously impede the learning process in a simulation. One such negative incident, documented by Leigh (2003a) shows the power of the 'gaze' as a disruptor of the simulation process. A participant's fears of 'being observed' derailed their capacity to learn in the environment created by a particular simulation and so dominated the process that it ended prematurely. All this was only uncovered, by chance, a year or so later, when it was discovered that fear of 'the gaze' of others was also connected to older physiological memories which (on this occasion) the participant consciously chose not to share.

The mutuality of the gaze can also reflect power structures, and even the nature of relationships between the subjects, as for example the proposition by Lutz and Collins (1993) that the gaze can even dictate terms under which individuals do/do not have rights or a need to look at others. Leigh (2003a) developed the idea of 'hovering invisibly' as a way of remaining out of the line of sight of participants without leaving the learning space. The practice emerged from noticing that some participants tried to observe the facilitator to gather cues and clues about how to behave in the simulation.

Given the complexity of this concept, there is clearly much to be learned by facilitators about how to manage the impact of observing participants during the action phase.

4 Contributions to Developing Facilitator Skills

As a 'container,' simulation for experiential learning has a permeable boundary through which many aspects of real life can seep as the activity progresses. The facilitator is responsible for maintaining—as far as possible—the integrity of the container, and for finding and applying a 'band aid' or effecting 'repairs' when and if there are breaches. Each of the four perspectives explored in the foregoing discussion can contribute to creating breaches in the container and facilitators need to be ever vigilant in watching for possible emergence of problems caused by any one of them (Leigh and Spindler 1998). The facilitator's capabilities and readiness for appropriate responses are an oft-forgotten commodity in regard to safety in simulations. Expert facilitators have moved along the spectrum from novice, to competent operator, to expert, while being shaped by their own sociological interconnected phenomenology and personal perspectives will have played their part in shaping their actions and behaviours in specific contexts. Facilitators—like all experts—grow into their role and, along with increasing expertise, comes acceptance that occasionally awareness of what is required may go in new directions as current mental models are expanded by new experiences in areas not previously encountered.

5 Concluding Comments

At this point in the research we know that there is much yet to learn about how to guide and inform novice facilitators, as well as providing experts with the kind of theoretical underpinnings that confirm their expertise. All four perspectives explored in this paper are significant tools for guiding future work. They are outside the usual list of per-spectives considered as relevant to facilitator knowledge and yet, as we have demon-strated, each one has enormous potential to influence—for better or worse—the participant experience of learning in simulation-based contexts. Future research can explore them further with more evidentiary cases and reconceptualise them as a holistic underpinning model for further thinking.

References

Benner, P.: From Novice to Expert: Excellence and Power in Clinical Nursing Practice, pp. 13–34. Addison-Wesley, Menlo Park (1984)

Carrera, A.M., et al.: Constructing safe containers for effective learning: vignettes of breakdown in psychological safety during simulated scenarios. In: Naweed, A., Wardaszko, M., Leigh, E., Meijer, S. (eds.) ISAGA/SimTecT -2016. LNCS, vol. 10711, pp. 15–29. Springer, Cham (2018). https://doi.org/10.1007/978-3-319-78795-4_2

Chandler, D.: Notes on 'The Gaze' (2014). http://visual-memory.co.uk/daniel/Documents/gaze/gaze02.html

Christopher, E.M., Smith, L.E.: Leadership Training Through Gaming: Power, People and Problem Solving. Kogan Page, London (1987)

Edmondson, A.C.: Managing the risk of learning: psychological safety in work teams. Citeseer (2002)

Eliason, N.: The Step-by-Step Guide to Go From Novice to Expert in Any Skill (2019). https://www.nateliason.com/blog/become-expert-dreyfus

Fuchs, T.: The phenomenology of body memory. Body Mem. Metaphor Mov. **84**, 9–22 (2012)

Gilbert, D.T., Wilson, T.D.: Why the brain talks to itself: sources of error in emotional prediction. Philos. Trans. R. Soc. B Biol. Sci. **364**(1521), 1335–1341 (2009)

Heeswijk, M.D.W.-V.: The role of the facilitator and ethics: don't take yourself too seriously, on the other hand do because you need to be a professional (2018)

International Association of Facilitators. IAF Core Competencies (2019). https://www.iaf-world.org/site/professional/core-competencies

Leigh, E.: A Practitioner Researcher Perspective on Facilitating an Open, Infinite, Chaordic Simulation. (EdD), University of Technology, Sydney (2003a). https://opus.lib.uts.edu.au/handle/2100/308

Leigh, E.: A touchy subject—people factors in simulations. Paper presented at the SimTECT 2003, Adelaide (2003b)

Leigh, E., Spindler, L.: Vigilant observer: a role for facilitators of games/simulations. In: Geurts, J., Joldersma, C., Roelofs, E. (eds.) Gaming/Simulation for Policy Development and Organizational Change. Tilburg University Press, Tilburg (1998)

Lutz, C., Collins, J.: Reading National Geographic. University of Chicago Press, Chicago (1993)

McIver, D.: Tayla Harris AFLW photo could become landmark moment in Australian sport (2019). https://www.abc.net.au/news/2019-03-21/tayla-harris-aflw-photo-could-be-landmark-moment-in-australia/10921892. Accessed 27 May 2019

Mezirow, J.: Transformative Dimensions of Adult Learning. JosseyBass, San Francisco (1991)

Radonyi, P., Leigh, E.: Assessment and evaluation of learning via simulation. In: Naweed, A., Wardaszko, M., Leigh, E., Meijer, S. (eds.) ISAGA/SimTecT -2016. LNCS, vol. 10711, pp. 116–133. Springer, Cham (2018). https://doi.org/10.1007/978-3-319-78795-4_9

Rudolph, J.W., Raemer, D.B., Simon, R.: Establishing a safe container for learning in simulation: the role of the presimulation briefing. Simul. Healthc. **9**(6), 339–349 (2014)

Safire, W.: On Language; Suspension of Disbelief. New York Times, 7 October 2007. https://www.nytimes.com/2007/10/07/magazine/07wwln-safire-t.html

Salas, E., Rosen, M.A., DiazGranados, D.: Expertise-based intuition and decision making in organizations. J. Manag. **36**(4), 941–973 (2010)

Scannell, E.: Games Trainers Play. McGraw Hill, New York (1980)

Thomas, G.: A Studty of the Theories and Practices of Facilitator Educators. La Trobe University, Melbourne (2007)

Torbert, W.R., Fisher, D.: Autobiographical awareness as a catalyst for managerial and organisational development. Manag. Educ. Dev. **23**(3), 184–198 (1992)

"For Your SA": Insights from a Situation Awareness Training Study

Alex McNaughton[1], Susannah J. Whitney[2(✉)], and Philip Temby[2]

[1] The University of Adelaide, North Terrace, Adelaide, SA 5000, Australia
alex.mcnaughton@sa.gov.au
[2] Defence Science and Technology,
Third Avenue, Edinburgh, SA 5111, Australia
{susannah.whitney, philip.temby}@dst.defence.gov.au

Abstract. Situation awareness (SA) is widely regarded to be important for task performance in complex environments. Endsley's (1995) model describes SA on three levels: perception, comprehension, and projection. There is considerable interest in improving SA, including through training interventions. In this paper we report on the results of a recent SA training study and identify some insights gained during this study. We developed and tested the efficacy of a brief training intervention, comprising rehearsal and feedback of SA probes, to enhance individual SA in a simulated reconnaissance mission. We compared the performance of two groups of participants, an experimental group (n = 11) who received the intervention, and a control group (n = 12) who did not receive the intervention. Contrary to prediction, training did not improve performance on objective and subjective measures of SA. We discuss our insights in terms of understanding, measuring and improving SA.

Keywords: Situation awareness · Training · Simulation

1 Introduction

Various occupations require personnel to work in complex operating environments with significant cognitive demands. Such work environments can place personnel at risk of making poor decisions with potentially catastrophic outcomes. In the military context, future operating environments will be characterized by increased uncertainty and complexity due to the changing nature of warfare (Australian Army 2014). To help mitigate against these demands, the Australian Army is seeking ways to prepare individuals to make effective decisions in challenging conditions (Department of Defence 2015).

Effective decision making in complex environments relies on good situation awareness (SA). Broadly speaking, SA is an awareness and understanding of what is going on in the environment. Better SA is associated with better task performance, while poorer SA, or a loss of SA, can lead to catastrophic system failures or near misses (Wright and Endsley 2008).

Given the importance of SA, there is considerable interest in methods for enhancing it. In this paper, we aim to highlight some key considerations in designing SA training

A. Naweed et al. (Eds.): ASC 2019, CCIS 1067, pp. 13–29, 2019.
https://doi.org/10.1007/978-981-32-9582-7_2

interventions. We use a case study approach, drawing on our insights from our own study of the effectiveness of a brief SA training intervention. We start with a broad overview of SA theory, followed by approaches for training SA. Next, we describe the methodology and results from our study. We conclude by discussing some of our insights and offering suggestions for future SA research.

1.1   Situation Awareness

One of the most influential and popular models of SA (Endsley 1995) suggests it comprises three levels:

1. Perception of objects in the environment,
2. Comprehension of the current situation, and
3. Projection of future status.

For example, a military commander receives information about the location of opposing forces (Level 1), identifies the likely tactics their opponents are employing (Level 2), and uses this knowledge to gain a tactical advantage (Level 3).

While popular, Endsley's model is not universally accepted (Flach 2015; Sarter and Woods 1991; Wickens 2008). Researchers continue to debate matters, including whether SA is a state or process, what comprises SA, how to measure SA, and practical implications of SA. While we are aware of this ongoing debate, it is beyond the scope of the paper to resolve it[1]. Our study is grounded in Endsley's theory. This theory is accepted within Army, and also underpins the majority of published interventions on SA training (see Table 1 and associated discussion in the following section).

Under Endsley's model, SA is influenced by (or perhaps comprised of) a range of variables that characterize differences between individuals, such as working memory, attentional capacity, and prior experience with the task of interest (Bender et al. 2018; Gutzwiller and Clegg 2013; Kaber et al. 2016; Redden 2001). SA may also be positively or negatively affected by the way the system is designed or the way it communicates information to operators (Endsley 1995).

Although it originated as a construct within the aviation industry, SA is now considered relevant to any domain where humans work with complex systems. This includes the military, health care, manufacturing, power plants, cybersecurity, and driving (Endsley 1995; van Winsen et al. 2015). Given the role SA plays in supporting performance in complex environments, exploring ways to enhance it have intuitive appeal.

There are three broad approaches to enhancing SA, which are not mutually exclusive (Kearns 2011). First, tasks, displays, and equipment can be specifically designed to support SA (Endsley 2016). Second, recruitment and selection processes can incorporate measures of SA to identify candidates with relevant abilities (Redden 2001). Third, training interventions can be developed and used to improve individual SA (Chancey and Bliss 2012; Endsley and Garland 2000).

---

[1] For further reading on this, we suggest Dekker (2015) and Endsley (2015).

In the case study, we chose to focus on a training intervention. Our decision was consistent with Army's broad strategic interest in improving the cognitive performance of individuals, including through redesigning training (Department of Defence 2015). Based on previous studies, which we discuss in the next section, we also believed that there was a sound evidence base for the efficacy of training interventions to enhance SA.

1.2 Training Situation Awareness

SA comprises a range of cognitive processes and several different approaches for training interventions have been employed. Most commonly, interventions either target the underlying cognitive processes, such as attention and memory, or provide opportunities to rehearse the task of interest (Endsley and Robertson 2000; Salas et al. 1995).

There is currently no consensus on whether SA training interventions should target specific levels of Endsley's model. On the surface, it may be intuitive to direct training interventions towards Level 1 SA. There is evidence from aviation accidents that Level 1 SA errors occur most frequently (Endsley and Garland 2000), and it seems reasonable to assume that individuals begin with Level 1 SA of their environment, and progress to Levels 2 and 3. However, there does not appear to be any systematic evidence from other industries on the relative frequencies of Level 1, 2, and 3 SA errors, and from a theoretical perspective, Endsley suggests that individuals do not necessarily start with Level 1 SA, and that it's not necessarily a prerequisite for Levels 2 and 3 SA (Endsley 2015; Stanton et al. 2017).

There are several different approaches for measuring SA, including:

- Objective measures, where respondents are asked factual questions, such as "what are the map coordinates of the nearest friendly asset?". Examples of this assessment type include the Situation Awareness Global Assessment Technique (SAGAT; Endsley 2017) and the Situation Present Awareness Method (SPAM; Durso and Dattel 2004).
- Self-rated SA, where respondents rate (self-report) their own level of SA (Strater et al. 2001; Taylor 2017).
- Observer ratings of SA, where experts or other participants rate an individual's SA (Carretta et al. 1996; Matthews and Beal 2002).
- Performance-based measure of SA, where actions during a task are assumed to reflect the respondent's level of SA; for example, go/no-go decisions, or number of targets correctly identified (Lehtonen et al. 2017; Saus et al. 2006).

Each of these measurement approaches has different underlying assumptions. For instance, objective assessments tend to rely on a respondent's memory of the scenario. Self-ratings assume that an individual can accurately perceive and evaluate their own SA. Observer ratings and performance-based measures assume that the cognitive processes associated with SA can be measured from observable behaviors. Given these differing assumptions, it is not surprising that there appears to be little correlation between different types of measurement approaches (Endsley et al. 1998; Endsley et al. 2000; Salmon et al. 2009). This suggests that multiple assessment types should be used, in order to obtain a more comprehensive picture of an individual's SA.

Irrespective of the type of intervention that is used, the levels of SA targeted, or the way SA is measured, it is possible to draw out some broad principles for the structure of SA training interventions. For instance, it is important to provide trainees with opportunities to rehearse the behaviors (Salas et al. 1995) or skills of interest. Structured feedback on performance is also vital for learning (Endsley and Robertson 2000). For safety and logistical reasons, it may be preferable to use simulation rather than the live environment (Redden 2001; Riley et al. 2009).

Drawing on these principles, a number of researchers have studied the impact of SA training interventions in complex simulation-based tasks. Some of the key studies are summarized in Table 1. The studies used a range of tasks, such as simulated flight, tactical decision-making, and air traffic control. Training interventions typically used some combination of briefings on the nature of SA, training on some of the foundational cognitive skills, rehearsing the task of interest, and rehearsing SA queries. The majority of these studies implicitly or explicitly used Endsley's (1995) model of SA, including using the SAGAT as an SA measure. While SAGAT was the most frequently used measure of SA, some studies used combinations of objective and subjective SA assessment.

Importantly, these studies generally – but not consistently – demonstrated that a brief training intervention was able to improve levels of SA. Most studies used training interventions that were around five to seven hours in duration (Bolstad et al. 2010; Burkolter et al. 2010; Gayraud et al. 2017), or took place over several days (Gonzalez and Wimisberg 2007; Sarter and Woods 1991). However, a number of studies demonstrated significant improvement in SA with interventions as short as 20 to 90 min (Kearns 2011; Lehtonen et al. 2017; O'Brien and O'Hare 2007).

Table 1. Summary of SA training studies

Study	Participants	SA training intervention	SA measure	Results
Bolstad et al. (2010)	24 pilots	Seven hours rehearsing flight checklist completion, comprehension and psychomotor skills	SAGAT probes during simulated flight	Significant improvement on two out of fifteen SAGAT queries
Burkolter et al. (2010)	47 undergraduate engineering students	Five hours, including briefing on Endsley's model of SA, rehearsing SAGAT probes and practicing SA task	SAGAT probes during simulated cabin management task	Significant improvement in diagnosing system faults, but no overall improvement in SA
Gayraud et al. (2017)	12 pilot trainees	Five hours, including briefings on SA, discussions of case studies, and completion of subjective SA measurement	SAGAT probes during simulated flight	Higher SAGAT scores in pilots receiving training, but not statistically significant

(*continued*)

Table 1. (*continued*)

Study	Participants	SA training intervention	SA measure	Results
Gonzalez and Wimisburg (2007)	36 adults	Over three days, participants rehearsed a control room simulation with embedded SA probes. Half the participants could view system status info during probes, half could not	SAGAT probes during control room simulation	SAGAT scores improved over time, but only for participants who could not view system status during probes
Kearns (2011)	36 pilots	90 min, not described in detail	SAGAT probes during simulated flight	Significantly higher SAGAT scores for pilots who received training
Lehtonen et al. (2017)	36 children and 22 adults	15–20 min. Participants viewed video footage of a cyclist travelling through a city. At various points the footage was paused and masked, and participants were asked to identify locations of potential hazards	SAGAT probes while watching video footage	Accuracy significantly increased over time
O'Brien and O'Hare (2007)	28 university students	90 min across three sessions, rehearsing air traffic control simulation with specific guidance on attention management and maintaining three levels of SA	Performance on air traffic control simulation without guidance	Training significantly improved performance for participants with low SA ability, participants with high SA ability performed well irrespective of whether or not they received training
Saus et al. (2006)	40 police academy trainees	Brief intervention, exact time not specified, rehearsing SAGAT-style probes in simulator with structured debriefing	Two self-report questionnaires following simulated shoot-don't shoot scenarios, observer ratings of SA, performance in simulator scenarios	Participants receiving training had significantly higher self-rated and observer-rated SA and significantly better performance in the simulator scenarios
Strater et al. (2004)	80 military cadets	Between 20 min and 8 h completing computer-based military missions incorporating SAGAT probes and feedback	SAGAT probes, self-assessed SA, and tactical decision-making during field exercise	Considerable missing data points, but some significant differences on SAGAT queries between participants who did and did not receive training

The intervention that produced significant improvements in SA in the shortest duration (around 20 min) was in the study conducted by Lehtonen et al. (2017). In this study, participants viewed first-person perspective video footage of a cyclist riding through a busy city. Participants completed 30 hazard identification trials, where the screen was blanked, and they were asked to identify the location of various hazards, such as an oncoming vehicle or pedestrian about to step into traffic. There was no standalone training intervention; instead, researchers examined the effects of training by comparing performance over time. The researchers divided responses into three blocks of 10 trials ("start", "middle phase", and "end") and compared performance over time. They found that participants showed significantly improved accuracy and decreased response time between the start and the end (i.e., the first 10 trials and the final 10 trials).

Military personnel may have limited time to take part in training interventions. If they can improve their SA on relevant tasks in as little as 20 min, as suggested by Lehtonen et al. (2017), this has considerable practical utility for this population. However, one key limitation of Lehtonen et al's study was that there was no test of transfer; participants were not tested to see if the improvements gained during training were evident in a different context.

We have previously reported results from a study looking at SA in a simulated reconnaissance task (Hibbard et al. 2018). While the focus of Hibbard's study was on the impact of simulation display (flatscreen vs VR) and background briefing style, a key finding was that, irrespective of experimental condition, participants were able to identify and comprehend the meaning and implication of events and objects in their environment. That is, participants demonstrated Level 1 and Level 2 SA. We used the same scenarios used by Hibbard to test our training intervention.

The current study aimed to test if a brief SA training intervention, based around rehearsing the task of interest, produced improvements in individual SA during training and in a transfer task. It was predicted that participants receiving SA training would demonstrate improved SA (as measured through objective and subjective measures) relative to participants not receiving SA training.

2   Method

The study employed a 2 × 2 mixed design. The between-subjects factor was training condition (experimental vs control) and the within-subjects factor was time (Mission 1 vs Mission 2). The study received ethics approval from low risk ethics panels in Defence Science and Technology and the University of Adelaide.

2.1   Participants

Participants were 23 university students and defence civilian employees (16 men, 7 women), aged 18 to 40 years (M = 27.39 years, SD = 4.95 years). They were recruited using a combination of printed and online promotional material, and word of mouth (i.e., convenience and snowball sampling). Participants were randomly assigned to an experimental (n = 11) or control (n = 12) condition.

2.2   Materials

Simulated Reconnaissance Task
Participants played the role of a fictional civilian aid worker operating in a military environment. Their primary role was to drive a simulated vehicle and pay attention to any unusual activity in the surrounding environment as part of a reconnaissance and humanitarian mission. They were given printed briefing materials to read that described the security situation and identified friendly, opposing, and civilian personnel operating in the environment.

The task comprised two discrete missions within the virtual environment. In Mission 1, participants were asked to drive along a designated route to deliver medical supplies from a UN base to a nearby hospital. In Mission 2, participants were asked to make the return journey from the hospital to the base. Traffic signs and road barriers were used to provide navigational assistance; participants were not required to make complex choices about route selection.

Along the route, there were a number of noteworthy events, such as police and civilians standing alongside a helicopter, or the aftermath of an IED detonation. In some cases, these events were consistent with the information provided in the background briefing. However, there were also events which suggested that there were inaccuracies in, or changes to, the security situation outlined in the initial briefing. The briefing also asked participants to report any changes in the security situation or any other events of interest.

The simulated reconnaissance task and missions were conducted using the software Virtual Battlespace Systems 3 (VBS3), and a driving simulator comprising computer, keyboard, mouse, and flatscreen monitor. These missions and accompanying briefing material are described in more detail in Hibbard et al. (2018).

2.3   Measures

In this study, we used a combination of objective and subjective measures of SA. We believed this would result in a more comprehensive assessment of SA than using only a single measure. These were different measures to those used in Hibbard et al. (2018) as the two studies had different objectives. Hence it is not possible to directly compare the findings from this study to those obtained by Hibbard et al.

Objective SA
The SAGAT (Endsley 2017) is an objective measure of SA. It is intended to directly assess respondents' knowledge of their environment, by freezing the simulation and asking them to answer factual questions. In our study, SAGAT probes were used to assess Level 1 and 2 SA. Sample questions included:

- Since leaving Camp Amy what average speed have you been travelling?
- Did you encounter any vehicles since leaving Camp Amy?
- Approximately how long in minutes has it been since you left Camp Amy?
- Did you encounter any Sahrani military personnel? If yes, were they carrying weapons?

Correct answers were given a score of 1, and incorrect answers were scored 0. Partially correct answers were given a fractional score. For instance, correctly identifying that Sahrani military personnel had been encountered, but incorrectly identifying that they were unarmed, received a score of 0.5. Scores for each probe were summed to give a total score for Level 1 and Level 2 SA. Higher total scores indicated higher SA.

Subjective SA

The Post-Trial Situation Awareness Questionnaire (PSAQ; Strater et al. 2001) is a self-report measure of SA. It comprises three questions, asking participants to rate their workload, performance, and awareness of the situation on a scale from 1 (lowest) to 5 (highest). Responses to the three questions are added together to generate a total score, ranging from 3 to 15. Higher scores indicate higher self-rated SA.

2.4 Procedure

Participants were tested individually in a quiet, laboratory environment. On arrival, they were given an introductory briefing on the study and gave informed consent to participate. Following this, they practiced driving in the virtual world until they reported that they were familiar with the system controls; while not formally timed or controlled, this took less than five minutes for all participants.

Next, participants were given a briefing and completed Mission 1. At three checkpoints in the simulated environment, identified by yellow roadside markers, participants stopped to complete SAGAT probes. The number of SAGAT probes at each checkpoint ranged from five to seven, with a total of 21 probes in Mission 1, and 15 in Mission 2. Administering the SAGAT at specific, non-random times during the mission is consistent with previous studies of SA in military contexts (Chancey and Bliss 2012). When participants reached their destination at the end of each mission, they completed the PSAQ.

SA Training Intervention

Following Mission 1, participants in the control condition played a computer game (Tetris) for 30 min. Participants in the experimental condition completed a 30-min SA training intervention. This comprised seven trials, each consisting of a still image or brief video segment (30 s maximum) of pre-recorded VBS3 footage. Prior to viewing the footage, participants were instructed that they would be tested on their ability to perceive and comprehend relevant elements in the environment. After viewing the footage, participants completed multiple-choice SAGAT probe questions measuring Level 1 and Level 2 SA and were given feedback on their responses.

Figure 1 is one of the still images used in the SA training intervention. After viewing this image, participants were asked questions such as:

- (Level 1 SA) What was the name of the area displayed on the road sign?
- (Level 1 SA) What type of vehicle is the military vehicle pictured in the image? (Options included tank, medical vehicle, combat vehicle, and unknown)
- (Level 2 SA) Based on your understanding of the elements in the picture, what do you think is most likely happening in this scene? (Response options included lunch break, medical emergency, and unknown).

Fig. 1. Sample image from Situation Awareness training intervention

Each trial included between one and three Level 1 SA probes and one or two Level 2 SA probes (except for the first trial, where only Level 1 probes were used)[2].

At the conclusion of the training intervention, or game playing interval, all participants completed Mission 2, with SA measures administered as per Mission 1. Each mission took approximately 20 min to complete, depending on driving speed. The total duration of the experiment was approximately 70–80 min.

3   Results

3.1   Objective SA

Mean SAGAT scores for Mission 1 and Mission 2 for both groups are shown in Fig. 2. The raw scores have been converted to percentages to facilitate comparisons. Error bars in this, and all other figures, indicate the Standard Error of the Mean.

As shown in the figure, in both conditions, there was a slight decrease in mean SAGAT scores from Mission 1 to Mission 2, but no discernible difference in SAGAT scores between the experimental and control groups.

A 2×2 ANOVA confirmed that there were no significant main effects or interactions. The effect of training condition was non-significant, $F(1, 21) = 0.2$, $p = .66$, with a small effect size, $\eta2 = .01$. No other main or interaction effects (time and condition) were found to be statistically significant ($p > .05$).

To determine if the training had differential effects on different levels of SA, the Level 1 and Level 2 SAGAT probes were reanalyzed separately. These additional analyses confirmed that there were no significant effects or interactions for Level 1 or Level 2 probes.

---

[2] In our study, Level 3 probes (i.e., questions pertaining to projection of future status) were not used due to the specific nature of the missions; hence no Level 3 data is reported.

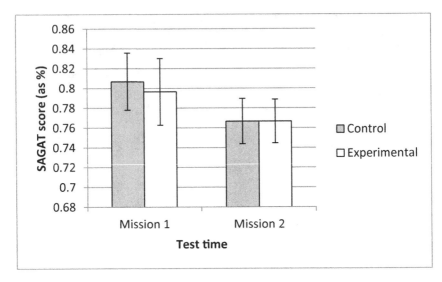

Fig. 2. SAGAT scores

3.2   Subjective SA

PSAQ scores for Mission 1 and Mission 2 for both groups of participants are shown in Fig. 3. As shown in the figure, in both conditions, scores decreased slightly between Mission 1 and Mission 2, and scores for participants in the experimental condition were slightly lower than scores for participants in the control condition.

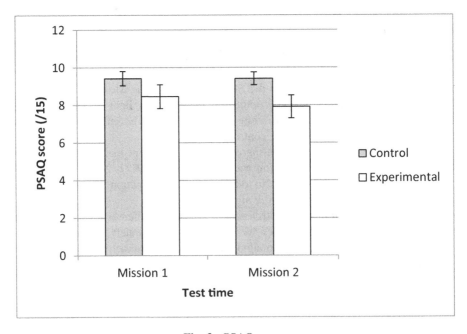

Fig. 3. PSAQ scores

A 2 × 2 mixed ANOVA found the effect of training condition approached levels of significance, $F(1, 21) = 3.46$, $p = .08$, with a small effect size, $\eta2 = .01$. The effect of time was non-significant, $F(1, 21) = 1.34$, $p = .26$, with a large effect size, $\eta2 = .14$. The interaction between training and time was also non-significant, $F(1, 21) = 0.85$, $p = .26$.

As the effect of training approached significance, the Mission 1 and Mission 2 PSAQ scores were separately analyzed using independent samples t-tests. Results indicated that following training, PSAQ scores in the experimental group were significantly lower than the control group, $t(21) = 2.22$, $p = .04$. Closer examination of the three questions comprising the PSAQ indicated that responses differed significantly for only one question, self-rated performance. Participants in the experimental condition gave significantly lower scores for this question than participants in the control condition, $t(21) = 2.35$, $p < .05$. Scores for the other two questions on the PSAQ did not differ significantly between conditions.

As an additional analysis, the correlation between SAGAT and PSAQ scores was calculated. The result was a small, non-significant correlation, $r = -.07$, $p = .74$.

3.3 SA Training Data

Data from the SA training intervention was unavailable for one participant, so the data reported in this section is based on the remaining 10 participants in the experimental condition.

Figure 4 shows the mean percentage score for Level 1 and Level 2 SA queries in each trial (there were no Level 2 queries in the first trial). As the figure shows, accuracy for Level 1 SA started out low, but increased across trials. In contrast, accuracy for Level 2 SA remained high across trials with only small fluctuations.

The changes in scores over trials were analyzed using two repeated-measures ANOVAs, one for Level 1 probes and the other for Level 2 probes. Results from these

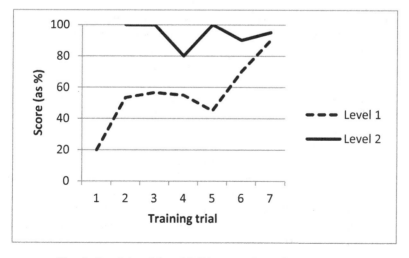

Fig. 4. Level 1 and Level 2 SA scores for each training trial

analyses confirmed that the effects of trial were significant for Level 1 SA, F (6, 54) = 7.32, $p < .001$, and Level 2 SA, F (5, 45) = 2.87, $p < .05$.

4   Discussion and Conclusions

The aim of this case study was to test the efficacy of a brief training intervention on individual SA in the context of a simulated reconnaissance task. We predicted that the intervention would be effective, based on previous research on SA training interventions, the use of recommended training principles such as feedback and rehearsal, and results from our previous study using the same briefing materials and scenarios. On balance, the results did not demonstrate that the training intervention was effective. Three key findings from this study were:

First, participants who received SA training showed improved accuracy in responding to SAGAT probes during the intervention, consistent with results reported by Lehtonen et al. (2017).

Second, improvements in performance during the training intervention did not result in transfer of training to objective SA during Mission 2. This was contrary to our expectations, although as noted in Table 1, there are also several previous studies where SA training did not significantly improve performance (e.g. Bolstad et al. 2010; Burkolter et al. 2010).

Third, the only change in SA following training was a significant decrease in subjective SA. As a corollary, there was no significant relationship between objective and subjective SA, which is consistent with previous research (Endsley et al. 1998; Endsley et al. 2000; Salmon et al. 2009).

The significant change in performance in the training intervention suggests that some learning was occurring. However, despite the apparent similarities between the activities in the training intervention and the post-Mission objective SA queries, there did not appear to be any training transfer. One possible explanation is a number of subtle but important differences between the training and test protocols.

In training, participants viewed footage for 15–30 s with SA queries following immediately afterwards. In contrast, during the missions, participants drove in the virtual environment for 6–7 min before responding to the SA probes. This may have resulted in differences between the amount of information participants needed to notice and remember, and the salience of the items used for the SA probes.

To illustrate this, consider Fig. 1, one of the images used in the SA training intervention. There are only a small number of objects in the figure, and it is possible that with practice, participants could reasonably guess which elements were most likely to feature in the SA probes and maintain relevant information in memory for a short time. In contrast, consider the Level 1 and Level 2 SA probes used during Mission 1 and Mission 2 (see Sect. 2.3). Information required to answer these probes may not always have been highly salient. For instance, participants may not have been easily able to count and remember the number of vehicles encountered, or to keep track of the elapsed time since leaving the departure point, notwithstanding that they were instructed to monitor their surroundings.

Results from previous studies provide some support for this explanation. Previous research has highlighted the importance of memory and attentional control in supporting SA (Bender et al. 2018; Gonzalez and Wimisberg 2007; Gutzwiller and Clegg 2013; Kaber et al. 2016). Furthermore, Gonzalez and Wimisberg suggest that "the impact of practice on SA… depends on how SA is measured" (pp. 67–68). In their study, SA training only improved SA for participants who could not see the current system status during SA probes. Participants who were able to view the system status during probes showed no improvement. In addition, Bender et al. suggest an individual's ability to remember SA-relevant information is shaped by their ability to control attention towards this information.

Related to the issue of salience, it is possible that the SA probes during Mission 1 and Mission 2 were not sufficiently linked to the primary objective. During the missions, participants were required to navigate through the virtual environment. However, this was a relatively straightforward task due to the provision of on-screen signs and waypoints. Participants were not required to choose their own route, and were not required to make any deviations from the signposted route, even when encountering events that were later the subject of SA probes. Although participants were instructed to maintain awareness of their environment and report any deviations from the security situation briefed at the outset of the mission, there were no other strong or intrinsically motivating factors to ensure that they maintained good SA throughout the missions, or distractors embedded in the task to test their ability to maintain SA.

Potentially, participants may have had more motivation to maintain SA if events forced them to make a decision, or where there were potential consequences for their ability to achieve their primary objective[3]. Examples may have been, if they could not follow their original route due to a road closure, were forced to take evasive action due to another vehicle's erratic driving, or were under sudden time pressure to find the fastest route to their destination. This may have been more consistent with previous studies of SA training interventions, where there was a stronger link between the primary objective of the complex task and the SA probes. For instance, in Saus et al.'s (2006) study of police trainees and Strater et al.'s (2004) study of military cadets, the primary objective was to make tactical decisions, and the SA queries related to tactics, planning, and decision-making.

The significant decrease in self-rated SA, and the lack of significant correlation with objective SA also merits some discussion. Previous studies have also failed to find significant relationships between subjective and objective measures of SA (Endsley et al. 1998; Endsley et al. 2000; Salmon et al. 2009). Researchers tend to explain these findings by suggesting that different types of SA measures tap into different processes or components of SA – which may account for the lack of significant correlations in this study – or that people cannot accurately judge or self-assess their own SA.

The suggestion that people cannot accurately self-assess SA may explain why subjective SA decreased following training. Potentially, the feedback provided during training (i.e., accuracy of response) helped participants in this condition more

---

[3] Using embedded events within training scenarios to trigger desirable behaviors is consistent with the Events-Based Approach to Training (EBAT) methodology (Fowlkes et al. 1998).

realistically assess and understand their performance. In doing so, they may have recalibrated their confidence level and rated their SA lower on subsequent measures. This explanation is supported by a recent SA study, which demonstrated that providing feedback on performance can help reduce overconfidence, defined as the difference between objective and subjective SA (Visser et al. in press).

The study limitations may also explain some of the lack of significant or expected findings. A sample size of 23 participants may have been too small for any genuine effects to be detected[4]. Also, the use of a civilian sample, rather than military personnel, may have meant that participants did not have sufficient experience or motivation with the task. These limitations should be addressed in future studies.

4.1 Insights for SA Training Research

While the current study examined individual SA on a simulated reconnaissance task, we believe the findings have broader utility for researchers. Based on our insights from this study, we offer the following suggestions for future SA research.

Conceptualizing and Defining SA: SA is a multidimensional construct, which appears to comprise a range of different cognitive processes, and to be influenced by a range of individual differences such as working memory, attentional control, and experience. Researchers should identify the theoretical model of SA they use, the specific aspects of SA that are of interest, and the specific processes that contribute to SA. For instance, we aimed to target Endsley's Level 1 SA (perception) by focusing on perception and comprehension of relevant objects in the environment.

Designing SA Measures: SA measures are typically embedded in, or linked to, a primary task. Items used for objective SA probes need to be salient, so that participants perceive them, and relevant to the primary task, so that participants interact with them to achieve specific task and or training objectives. However, there should also be scope for a range of responses depending on participants' individual differences – ceiling or floor effects should be avoided. In addition, SA measures should aim to be specific and not confounded by extraneous contributing factors.

While our prior research suggested the SA probes would be sufficiently salient, they may not have been sufficiently important to participants, or there may be have confounds due to memory.

Designing SA Training Interventions: An SA training intervention should address the specific cognitive processes of SA that are of interest to the study. It should also have a strong theoretical and conceptual rationale for expecting the intervention to produce improvement. Any potential confounds should also be reduced or removed. In addition, researchers should give due consideration to factors that will likely promote positive transfer of training (see Ford et al. 2018 for a review). Our study drew on previous successful training interventions (Lehtonen et al. 2017), and recommendations for training research (e.g. Salas et al. 1995). It also targeted specific cognitive

---

[4] Although our previous study using these materials (Hibbard et al. 2018) demonstrated significant effects with 14–15 participants per condition.

processes, attention and comprehension. However, as discussed in the preceding point, there may have been confounds due to the requirement to remember information.

Measuring SA: Different types of SA measures may yield different results, as evidenced by our differing findings using objective and subjective SA measures. The choice of measurement technique (and associated measures) should take into account the specific aspects or processes of SA that are of interest to the study, such as the use of Level 1 and Level 2 SAGAT probes to assess perception and comprehension. Alternatively, as suggested by previous researchers, multiple measurement techniques may be used for a more comprehensive assessment of SA.

In closing, we believe that we have identified some challenges associated with understanding, measuring, and improving SA. Our insights into these challenges, and how to address them, may help researchers and simulation practitioners in their respective fields.

Acknowledgements. Alex McNaughton completed this study in partial fulfilment of the degree of Master of Psychology (Organisation and Human Factors). He received a scholarship from the Department of Defence to support his research. Alex is now employed by the South Australian government. The briefing materials and scenarios used in the study were developed by Sarah Hibbard and Luke Thiele. The training material was developed with assistance from Ryan Dummin.

References

Australian Army: Future Land Warfare Report 2014. Commonwealth of Australia, Canberra (2014)

Bender, A.D., Loft, S.D., Lipp, O.V., Bowden, V.K., Whitney, S.J., Visser, T.A.W.: implications for army training and selection. In: Defence Human Sciences Symposium, Perth, WA (2018)

Bolstad, C.A., Endsley, M.R., Costello, A.M., Howell, C.D.: Evaluation of computer-based situation awareness training for general aviation pilots. Int. J. Aviat. Psychol. **20**(3), 269–294 (2010)

Burkolter, D., Kluge, A., Sauer, J., Ritzmann, S.: Comparative study of three training methods for enhancing process control performance: emphasis shift training, situation awareness training, and drill and practice. Comput. Hum. Behav. **26**(5), 976–986 (2010)

Carretta, T.S., Perry Jr., D.C., Ree, M.J.: Prediction of situational awareness in F-15 pilots. Int. J. Aviat. Psychol. **6**(1), 21–41 (1996)

Chancey, E.T., Bliss, J.P.: Unreliable information in infantry situation awareness: improvement through game-based training. Simul. Gaming **43**(5), 581–599 (2012)

Dekker, S.W.A.: The danger of losing situation awareness. Cogn. Technol. Work **17**(2), 159–161 (2015)

Department of Defence: Army Research and Development Plan. Commonwealth of Australia, Canberra (2015)

Durso, F.T., Dattel, A.: SPAM: the real-time assessment of SA. In: Banbury, S., Trembley, S. (eds.) A Cognitive Approach to Situation Awareness: Theory, Measures, and Application, pp. 137–154. Aldershot, New York (2004)

Endsley, M.R.: Toward a theory of situation awareness in dynamic systems. Hum. Factors J. Hum. Factors Ergon. Soc. **37**(1), 32–64 (1995)

Endsley, M.R., Selcon, S.J., Hardiman, T.D., Croft, D.G.: A comparative analysis of SAGAT and SART for evaluations of situation awareness. In: Proceedings of the Human Factors and Ergonomics Society Annual Meeting. SAGE Publications, Los Angeles (1998)

Endsley, M.R., Garland, D.J.: Proceedings of the Human Factors and Ergonomics Society Annual Meeting, vol. 44, SAGE Publications, Los Angeles (2000)

Endsley, M.R., Robertson, M.M.: Training for situation awareness in individuals and teams. In: Endsley, M.R., Garland, D.J. (eds.) Situation Awareness Analysis and Measurement, pp. 349–366. Lawrence Erlbaum, Mahwah (2000)

Endsley, M.R., Sollenberger, R., Stein, E.: Situation awareness: a comparison of measures. In: Proceedings of the Human Performance, Situation Awareness and Automation: User-Centered Design for the New Millennium, pp. 15–19 (2000)

Endsley, M.R.: Situation awareness misconceptions and misunderstandings. J. Cogn. Eng. Decis. Mak. 9(1), 4–32 (2015)

Endsley, M.R.: Designing for Situation Awareness: An Approach to User-Centered Design. CRC Press, Boca Raton (2016)

Endsley, M.R.: Direct measurement of situation awareness: validity and use of SAGAT. In: Salas, E. (ed.) Situational Awareness, pp. 129–156. Routledge, New York (2017)

Flach, J.M.: Situation awareness: context matters! A commentary on Endsley. J. Cogn. Eng. Decis. Mak. 9(1), 59–72 (2015)

Ford, J.K., Baldwin, T.T., Prasad, J.: Transfer of training: the known and the unknown. Annu. Rev. Organ. Psychol. Organ. Behav. 5, 201–225 (2018)

Fowlkes, J., Dwyer, D.J., Oser, R.L., Salas, E.: Event-based approach to training (EBAT). Int. J. Aviat. Psychol. 8(3), 209–221 (1998)

Gayraud, D., Matton, N., Tricot, A.: Efficiency of a situation awareness training module in initial pilot training. In: 19th International Symposium on Aviation Psychology (2017)

Gonzalez, C., Wimisberg, J.: Situation awareness in dynamic decision making: effects of practice and working memory. J. Cogn. Eng. Decis. Mak. 1(1), 56–74 (2007)

Gutzwiller, R.S., Clegg, B.A.: The role of working memory in levels of situation awareness. J. Cogn. Eng. Decis. Mak. 7(2), 141–154 (2013)

Hibbard, S.J., Whitney, S.J., Carter, L., Fidock, J.J.T., Temby, P., Thiele, L.: Making virtual sense: display type and narrative medium influence sensemaking in virtual environments. In: Naweed, A., Wardaszko, M., Leigh, E., Meijer, S. (eds.) ISAGA/SimTecT 2016. LNCS, vol. 10711, pp. 222–236. Springer, Cham (2018). https://doi.org/10.1007/978-3-319-78795-4_16

Kaber, D., Jin, S., Zahabi, M., Pankok Jr., C.: The effect of driver cognitive abilities and distractions on situation awareness and performance under hazard conditions. Transp. Res. Part F Traffic Psychol. Behav. 42, 177–194 (2016)

Kearns, S.: Online single-pilot resource management: assessing the feasibility of computer-based safety training. Int. J. Aviat. Psychol. 21(2), 175–190 (2011)

Lehtonen, E., Airaksinen, J., Kanerva, K., Rissanen, A., Ränninranta, R., Åberg, V.: Game-based situation awareness training for child and adult cyclists. R. Soc. Open Sci. 4(3), 160823 (2017)

Matthews, M.D., Beal, S.A.: Assessing Situation Awareness in Field Training Exercises. US Army Research Institute for the Behavioral and Social Sciences, Alexandria (2002)

O'Brien, K., O'Hare, D.: Situational awareness ability and cognitive skills training in a complex real-world task. Ergonomics 50(7), 1064–1091 (2007)

Redden, E.A.: Measuring and understanding individual differences in the situation awareness of workers in high-intensity jobs. Auburn University, Alabama (2001)

Riley, J.M., Scielzo, S., Hyatt, J., Davis, F., Colombo, D.: Situation awareness and performance feedback toward enhancing learning with game trainers: an approach and lessons learned. In: Proceedings of the Human Factors and Ergonomics Society Annual Meeting. Sage Publications Sage, Los Angeles (2009)

Salas, E., Prince, C., Baker, D.P., Shrestha, L.: Situation awareness in team performance: Implications for measurement and training. Hum. Factors J. Hum. Factors Ergon. Soc. 37(1), 123–136 (1995)

Salmon, P.M., et al.: Measuring Situation Awareness in complex systems: comparison of measures study. Int. J. Ind. Ergon. 39(3), 490–500 (2009)

Sarter, N.B., Woods, D.D.: Situation awareness: a critical but ill-defined phenomenon. Int. J. Aviat. Psychol. 1(1), 45–57 (1991)

Saus, E.-R., Johnsen, B.H., Eid, J., Riisem, P.K., Andersen, R., Thayer, J.F.: The Effect of brief situational awareness training in a police shooting simulator: an experimental study. Mil. Psychol. 18(S), S3 (2006)

Strater, L.D., Endsley, M.R., Pleban, R.J., Matthews, M.D.: Measures of Platoon Leader Situation Awareness in Virtual Decision-Making Exercises. US Army Research Institute for the Behavioral and Social Sciences, Alexandria (2001)

Strater, L.D., Reynolds, J.P., Faulkner, L.A., Birch, D.K., Hyatt, J.: PC-Based Training to Improve Infantry Situation Awareness. US Army Research Institute for the Behavioral and Social Sciences, Arlington, VA (2004)

Taylor, R.: Situational awareness rating technique (SART): the development of a tool for aircrew systems design. In: Salas, E. (ed.) Situational Awareness, pp. 111–128. Routledge, New York (2017)

van Winsen, R., Henriqson, E., Schuler, B., Dekker, S.W.: Situation awareness: some conditions of possibility. Theor. Issues Ergon. Sci. 16(1), 53–68 (2015)

Visser, T.A.W., et al.: Individual differences in higher-level cognitive abilities do not predict overconfidence in complex task performance. Consciousness and Cognition (in press)

Wickens, C.D.: Situation awareness: review of Mica Endsley's 1995 articles on situation awareness theory and measurement. Hum. Factors J. Hum. Factors Ergon. Soc. 50(3), 397–403 (2008)

Wright, M., Endsley, M.: Building shared situation awareness in healthcare settings. In: Nemeth, C.P. (ed.) Improving Healthcare Team Communication: Building Lessons from Aviation And Aerospace, pp. 97–114. Ashgate, Hampshire (2008)

Gaming Experience

Looking Good Sister! The Use of a Virtual World to Develop Nursing Skills

Pauletta Irwin[1]([✉]), Rosanne Coutts[2], and Iain Graham[2]

[1] University of Newcastle, Widderson Street, Port Macquarie, Australia
pauletta.irwin@newcastle.edu.au
[2] Southern Cross University, Lismore, Australia

Abstract. When developing contemporary nursing curricula the challenge is how to offer students a variety of authentic learning opportunities. Indeed, there is a generally held concern that the tertiary sector finds difficulty in achieving consistent, high quality opportunities for experiential learning. Additionally, these opportunities are often expensive and logistically problematic. A number of disciplines in higher education are opting for the use of contemporary software approaches that serve as valuable adjuncts for the delivery of learning content. This satisfies the students of today who demand experiences that are instantly gratifying, engaging and flexible. Nevertheless and contrastingly, the profession of nursing remains at its core a hands-on profession. Second Life is a three dimensional virtual world, that, due to its ability to promote collaborative, synchronous and immersive learning has been described as a rich social environment. Making decisions about how much technology should be included in the curriculum and at what point in the learner's journey it should be introduced presents a challenge to nurse educators. This research utilised a created nursing environment in Second Life where activities were embedded within three undergraduate nursing courses. All participating academics, and students were required to create their own avatar. Following the task, semi structured interviews were conducted, transcribed, coded and thematically analysed. The perspectives of practicing Registered Nurses and nursing academics and their students are presented. Observations, field notes and examination of relevant artefacts were also cyclically reviewed and incorporated. Findings from this research relate to the action of avatar creation within a pedagogical experience. It was established that offline characteristics influence a willingness to invest time and creativity when developing an online persona. Evidence of impression management was clear during customisation of the appearance and capabilities of the avatar. The findings suggest that there is relevance and transferability following participation in virtual world nursing experiences. Future investigation could focus on which students are best suited to learning this way and also what level of learning is actually achieved when in the role of a personalised 'ideal self avatar'.

Keywords: Avatar · Clinical practice · Connectivism · Education · Educational technology · Experiential learning · Nurse education · Second Life · Simulation · Virtual Worlds

© Springer Nature Singapore Pte Ltd. 2019
A. Naweed et al. (Eds.): ASC 2019, CCIS 1067, pp. 33–45, 2019.
https://doi.org/10.1007/978-981-32-9582-7_3

1 Introduction

The burgeoning of technologies used to augment student learning within conventional contexts continues to challenge those in higher education to rethink time honoured delivery methods. Indeed, the 'bricks and mortar' image evoked by the idea of higher-educational institutions is becoming outdated and these venerated establishments must move with the times. A new, digital learner, a global citizen, will thrive in a technologically supported education [1] where life experience is acknowledged as meaningful and the learning is authentic and readily applicable.

Fortuitously, Virtual Simulated Learning Environments (VSLEs), have features that can meet the expectations of these contemporary learners. VSLEs offer diverse applications across multiple disciplines [2] and are increasingly being utilised in higher education. Second Life (SL) is a three dimensional virtual world (VW) that can promote a rich social learning environment [3] with features that potentiate collaborative, synchronous, online learning [4].

1.1 Background

The tools of simulation are varied and range from low to high complexity and fidelity including mannequins, standardised patients, role-play and computer-generated simulations [5, 6]. Applied competently, one of the primary capabilities of simulated learning in nursing programs is to enhance the critical thinking and communication skills of undergraduates and of course ultimately, to improve the well-being and safety of their patients [7, 8]. This is achieved by providing students with the opportunity to rehearse both rare and regular clinical learning events in a safe, controllable environment.

Technological advances have furthered the diverse opportunities afforded by simulated learning and the degree of participant immersion during the process. These advances marry well with the pedagogy of adult, learner-centred education and they also keep abreast with the interests of the many digital natives enrolling in undergraduate nursing programs [1]. Virtual simulation is at the forefront of a student-centred approach to learning. The uptake and use of digital technologies by educators more broadly mimics the growth of the World Wide Web and our dependence upon it. Learning via virtual simulations is considered to be an extremely flexible, conducive and worthwhile educational option as it potentiates consumer technological dependence and ultimately challenges traditional notions of what learning at a higher education institutes should look like [9].

Gregory et al. [10] describe VWs as being flexible and able to provide an opportunity for heightened user engagement. Due to improved capacity and connectivity, VWs such as Open Sim, Unity 3D and Minecraft, have evolved markedly since their inception. SL's utilisation in higher education learning spaces has been showcased across multiple disciplines with its uptake being attributed to institutional desire and academic perseverance [11].

Research examining students' actions in and responses to, learning in a simulated environment such as SL, report profound immersion and describe their display of authentic behaviours that resemble real-world actions [6, 12]. The synchronous and asynchronous capabilities of this VW are congruent with the culture of contemporary higher education where learners divide time between life and learning commitments regardless of geographical constraints and the need to navigate the logistics of various schedules [13].

2 Theoretical Foundation: Connectivism

The historical and continued dominance of behaviourism, constructivism and cognitivism clearly remain relevant to the process of contemporary education as they still provide foundational theoretical support to many curricula in nursing programs. The concept of connectivism however, derives from a determination to address the entrenched inconsistencies in the application of these modern learning theories to contemporary, adult education [14]. The effect of technology upon the dynamics between learner and educator meant that established learning theories such as behaviourism, cognitivism and constructivism had limitations when applied within the field of adult education [15, 16]. Indeed Siemens [17] asserts that "technology has reorganised how we live, how we communicate and how we learn" (p. 5).

The pedagogical tenet of connectivism is a notion of connectedness between learners and whilst the technology itself is not a necessary component of the theory, the possibilities afforded by its use potentiate and augment knowledge connections [18]. Indeed, the idea that learning may reside in non-human appliances is a central principle of connectivism [16]. Beyond the connections between users, the strength in the knowledge and the continued growth of learning rests upon the diversity of opinions found in the users and the maintenance of veracity and cogency in the connections between them [14]. Clearly, there is little value in the undertaking, if every user has the same viewpoint or knowledge.

Boitshwarelo [18] acknowledges the literary consensus that views connectivism "as a fresh way of conceptualising learning in the digital age" (p. 161). Connectivism recognises the role of technology in providing a vast array of knowledge-connections via the internet which take place directly between the user (learner) and the knowledge source [17]. Further to this, according to Dunaway [17], learning takes place when the learner makes connections between concepts, ideas and beliefs to create new knowledge. However, in order to be a constructive undertaking, connectivism does require active learner engagement where astute, thoughtful search strategies result in siphoned information for new learner knowledge.

There is an ease of transition between formal and informal learning in a connectivist framework suggesting a need for adult learners to be intrinsically motivated, have confidence and an ability to initiate learning [19]. The high dependence on technology within a connectivist paradigm may leave those students who are not comfortable in the learning environment disenfranchised and marginalised [15, 19]. To achieve heightened levels of intrinsic motivation and therefore engagement, the user needs to feel a presence or belonging.

Presence. The idea of a learner's 'presence' is the subjective experience of being *in* an environment, regardless of physical location [19] and can include social and co-presence [20–22]. Bulu [20] suggests that the level of presence can be determined by an individual focusing on virtual stimulus in preference to the surrounding real life environment.

Social presence refers to the way in which the communication media can influence relationships through intimacy and immediacy. In the context of learning, comprehensive, individualised and timely feedback engenders social presence [23]. Where presence in general refers to *being in*, social presence refers to *being with*. Co-presence refers to the relationship potential at a psychological level. Co-presence in technology can be equated with interactions between peers where the commitment of both parties is to be approachable, available and accountable [20]. In their study, Tirado Morueta et al. [21] categorized social presence by demonstrated online affective, interactive and cohesive behaviours.

3   Research Methods

This research followed all ethical guidelines from the Southern Cross University Human Research and Ethics Committee (HREC) (Approval no. ECN-13-201). All participants in this research were invited by the researcher initially via an email communication.

3.1   Participants

The participants of this research were nursing academics as well as second year undergraduate nursing students. Although having different roles when in SL, both groups were included based on their ability to provide detailed descriptions about their experience and perceptions of interacting in a VW and of being exposed to content specific to nursing. Their participation was not dependent on age, gender or area of expertise.

All academics teaching into the courses that utilised SL were required to actively deliver content using this virtual platform as well as complete student assessments. The use of SL was compulsory for students enrolled in the associated courses. All students enrolled in the second year courses for the Bachelor of Nursing (BN) were required to utilise SL and to complete assessments.

3.2   Setting

A regional tri-campus higher education institute served as the setting for this research. The Australian Nurses and Midwifery Accreditation Council (ANMAC) had accredited each campus to deliver the BN degree and a conversion program (Diploma of Nursing to BN) that is delivered at one campus only. Equity standards dictate that each campus receive the same high-quality learning opportunities.

Virtual Setting

The computer-generated VW where the research took place was on three islands owned by the higher education institute in SL. In this VW users operate a self-created 3-dimensional representations of themselves known as avatars [3]. The avatar is capable of synchronous speech, text chat, gestures and movements such as walking and flying [6]. The outer layer of the avatar, the 'skin', can be manipulated at many levels of appearance including skin colour, head shape, eye shape and colour and body type.

Interaction Island is a virtual representation of the main campus of the higher education institute. Also, on this parcel of virtual land is a library, boardroom, gymnasium, open lecture theatre and sporting grounds. For the delivery of the BN, this area was used as a general virtual skill development area and as a formal (boardroom) and informal (courtyard) meeting space.

Commerce Town, another virtual space operated by the higher education institute, is a representation of a general community with a streetscape of various shops, a motel and an art gallery. The community setting also has a medical centre and an acute hospital ward where students participated in virtual patient assessments.

Education Island is predominantly used as a virtual learning space for another School within the higher education institute. That being written, there is a virtual house situated on this land parcel, which was utilised by one course in the BN curriculum where students conducted a home assessment.

Virtual Curricula

During the time of this research, SL was implemented in three courses within the BN during the second year of study.

Pain Assessment. Second year students took on the role of a community-based RN in SL as part of the compulsory course requirements. Upon entering the virtual community medical centre, as a nurse avatar, students were given a virtual notecard that informed them about the patient they were about to assess. Students were required to present their avatar in human form and be dressed as would be deemed appropriate for a nurse.

An academic operated the patient avatar and role-played this character for the entire assessment. The patient avatars were created to portray the associated social history. Examples of the patient scenarios included a biker gang member, an office worker and a manager of an international company.

When the pain assessment was completed, the academic would state "simulation end". At this point, the academic provided immediate feedback to the student in SL. To complete this phase of the simulation, the academic would change the appearance of their avatar to their own customised avatar. This new form more closely represented their real-world self.

Home Assessment. An additional course offered in first semester of the second year BN program gave students the option to use SL as the platform to record two simulated assessments. The assessment objectives were for students to demonstrate their ability to conduct a comprehensive assessment of clients based in the community and to conduct a hazard risk assessment.

Students could nominate to record interactions with an actor patient in real life (usually a friend or family member) or record interactions with an avatar patient in SL (again, usually operated by a family member or friend). To further enhance the realism of the virtual simulations, students were given instructions by way of a video clip that demonstrated how to make an 'older male' avatar that could be operated by their partner. Students were given instructions on how to purchase a new avatar 'skin' and then how to apply it to their own avatar. This provided information would assist students develop a more personalised avatar for the assessment.

Global Citizens. Students enrolled in the EN conversion course used SL as part of a compulsory graded assessment. Students worked in small inter-disciplinary/ international groups examining course content and prepared a presentation to be delivered in SL. Learning objectives for this virtual assessment aligned with the course objectives of gaining a broader understanding of global health and healthcare systems.

3.3 Research Design

Adaption of a multi method approach to data collection led to a rich understanding synonymous with a qualitative grounded approach. Data was collected incorporating observation, field notes, interviews and examination of artefacts.

Analysis of data commenced immediately after initial data collection. By being intentional and systematic in ongoing data collection and analysis, the researcher remained open to the investigation and examination of all cues that were relevant to the research. Data was collected and analysed in a cyclical manner that involved collection of data via observations, interviews and consideration of relevant artefacts such as course content and student results.

Analysis of this data would occur almost simultaneously as new data was then collected and analysed. The cyclical nature of the data collection and analysis as recommended by Corbin and Strauss [24], enabled the inclusion and exploration of newly identified relevant information with ensuing data collection. Saturation of data is readily apparent using this cyclical approach. Saturation occurs when continued collection of data reveals redundant content [25]. Saturation was considered as having occurred when new themes were not being revealed despite continued data collection.

4 Results

The following presents thematically grouped content that specifically relates to avatar creation. The assembled data in this category is comprised of participant interviews, researcher observations and reflections. Direct quotes from students and academics and research observations are used to personalise and contextualise the data.

Whilst receiving training and delivering feedback to students during learning activities, academics represented themselves with an avatar they had created. Findings about this align with the work of Mancini and Sibilla [26] where offline characteristics are often shown to be a starting point for avatar creation. Academics dressed their avatars (their 'skins') in business attire as is appropriate for a nursing academic.

As is common in real life, there were comments about what each other's avatar looked like, but these were limited to comments to a focus on hair styles and clothing choices. This reflects day to day interactions between colleagues suggesting a similar set of social norms were at play.

Further to this, several students created avatars that represented characteristics of themselves. This is clear in the following statement where the student describes 'dressing her up', it sounds almost like a reference to child's play or a maternal reference.

"I don't want to be someone else so that's why I dressed her up to look like me so I don't have to be someone else. It's just me going in there" (Student I).

Academics had patient avatars (skins) created for them to use when working with students in character. Patient avatar skins were designed by the virtual learning academic lead and represented a wide cross section of society. These represented varied age groups, ethnic backgrounds and social status.

All academics expressed enjoyment when 'being' their patient avatar for the first time. They were all interested to see what each other's avatar looked like and walked into each other's virtual assessment-come dressing rooms just to see what the other's appearance was. Most of them would do a twirl around and adopt the voice of the character they were role-playing and they would laugh. *"it was like they were excited children in a dress up shop" (Researcher field notes).*

Research field notes further denote various comments from academics regarding their approval about their patient avatar's appearance. Comments largely focussed on the attributes of the patient avatar; some were qualities that the academic did not possess in real life though would like, such as *"Check out my boobs" (Researcher field notes)* and others were attributes that the academic still wanted represented in their avatar and so made approving comments such as *"Good muscle tone" (Researcher field notes).*

All students were asked to create avatars that resembled human form and for their assessments, they were encouraged to wear nursing scrubs. Some students spoke about their avatars as though they were more than a representation of themselves but, rather, they were an extension. It was clear that the visual representation of the avatar enabled a strong sense of connection between avatar and owner. It is not surprising that the visual representation of the student's own avatar was important to them also.

Other students enjoyed the creative opportunity that building an avatar provided. Some students spoke of spending 'hours' creating their avatar profile. Interestingly, the following student refers to the avatar as a 'person' again suggesting an association or personal ownership between human and avatar and thus experiencing a sense of immersion in the activity. They said *"I enjoyed building my own person" (Student F).* This student provides an example that pre-dates the development of social or co-presence [20]. The learner demonstrates the connectedness of digital learning in its most innate form – connection with virtual self.

A particular academic told of a time about when she thought she would be role-playing a patient avatar named 'HokiSun' (who was from an Asian background). She had rehearsed an accent and particular actions to do in preparation for when in character. On the scheduled day, another academic had HokiSun's skin leaving the more rehearsed academic feeling disappointed because she had not prepared for another patient and she did not sense the same strong connection with 'them'.

Another academic explains an awkward moment that highlights feeling immersed when in SL and demonstrates self-presence.

"Yes, I did become immersed I did. I was surprised. Originally my avatar didn't have any clothes on and I actually felt really embarrassed (laughs). It surprised me. I do feel that I did become immersed. I cared about my avatar – you know what I was wearing" (Academic D).

This example also relays a belief that other learners in the environment, who witnessed the academic's 'nudity' would have a response that would warrant embarrassment. It suggests a social presence and a digital connection [18] where knowledge and expereinces are shared.

This level of belief was seen to have crossed the digital realm and into a 'reverse' reality for several academics such that they were behaving in real life as should the avatar in the VW. A particular academic spoke about role-playing a patient character with an arthritic knee. Her real life 'self' would rub her knee whilst her face would grimace.

Another academic spoke about being embarrassed by seeing a student's monster avatar groin. It is not clear whether this was an awkward moment for the academic because of a perceived inappropriate student-teacher relationship or if it was seeing the groin of another character. This speaks both to the transference of social norms to the virtual environment and the notion of social presence.

"Most people looked like a nurse um but one of them was so over the top you know like a monster with a tutu and (giggle) remember I was telling you about that and it he sat down .... yeah....and then there's this groin exposed and that's the camera view and...giggle...and then I had to look away from the screen because I couldn't do anything seriously looking at this character that was all...giggle...all hanging out and meant to be the nurse!" (Academic C).

Some of the academics describe what they believed to be examples of students being immersed or displaying social presence. One particular reflection shared by an academic demonstrates that the student avatar responded naturally, if not inappropriately for a nurse by forgoing any assessment measures and tending to the needs of the avatar patient.

"I remember once – obviously I was crying in the scenario and the poor student – without any assessment she rushed in and just wanted to fix it. And, of course, you don't get to find out their thinking until after it and she was like 'I just couldn't bear to see you in pain'. Which was a great lead in to say you always need to do an assessment. And then determine your actions – you know it was an acute care scenario" (Academic F).

Here, the student demonstrates immersion and presence by enacting perceivably real- world reactions to virtual events. Seo, Kim, Jung, Lee [27] describe this type of user online presence as when the "virtuality of self has become unnoticed" (p. 121). Several of the academics acknowledge that not only were many students' inworld behaviours appropriate for real-world responses but they matched the real- life persona of the student they had witnessed in the on campus classroom. In other words, they acted the same as their avatar.

Apart from demonstrating spatial awareness, witnessing socially polite gestures like apologising for bumping into each other, academics spoke about other common attributes that were represented in individual avatars. A confident and conscientious student translated to a confident avatar. Comparisons of results for the formative assessment (SL) and real life summative assessments for these students attests this notion. Whilst this same measure could generally be applied to those students who performed poorly, a number of academics spoke about students who lacked confidence when on campus with poor grades and who then transformed when in SL.

"She would come into the lab – she is pleasant, polite, superficial with others. A little bit socially inept at times but you could tell she was uncomfortable with her peers. And she did very, very, very well yeah.
Having that anonymity of the screen... To see a super different kid compared to her real life person. I definitely thought oh yes she was definitely different. There was a lot more to her once you scratched the surface with her. (Academic G).

Some academics tried to reason this behaviour given that some students performed *"better in the virtual environment than actually in the real-world" (Academic D)* by suggesting that SL provided a sheltered bridge to access the ability to perform appropriate nursing interventions and the conviction to make clinical reasoning decisions. The anonymity of the screen provided those lacking confidence the protection and self-belief to speak with others and confidently interview patients. It was observed that SL provided the bridge between on campus learning and practical experience.

"I think it gives them that confidence to speak to a patient. You know some of them have issues speaking with people and asking questions and I think, SL whilst it's not totally realistic it's realistic enough that makes it believable" (Academic G).

Perhaps a more poignant example of the strength SL gave to some students enabling a heightened learning experience is taken from the field notes during participant observation and the ensuing conversation with a student. These clearly demonstrate a change in learning style; from a real-world non-engaged student with no classroom participation to one of heightened engagement and enthusiasm. The situation depicts a student who was overweight, with hair that was not clean, body odour, wearing unironed clothing, and was non-participatory during on campus classes. This presentation of self was transformed inworld to dressing like a ninja warrior and dominating virtual discussions. When asked why the student was so vocal in SL, the student replied with the following:

"SL lets me be the me I want to be" (Researcher field notes).

This notion of a sheltered reality is pivoted when another student explains the value of learning using SL was a closer reflection of reality than on campus simulations. This student proposes that virtual simulations are a more realistic representation of their own nursing capability because they are acting as themselves through the purposeful actions of the avatar.

"I feel like in the labs if I had to role-play, you know come and consult with a patient, I feel silly because I am pretending" (Student D).

Visual and behavioural representations of self in SL were vast across the student group. Whilst there was an underlying element of fun for students, despite alternate looks and capability, students treated this learning with academic earnest. Perceptions of people who use inworld gaming are often nerds or as deviant because of the 'adult' content that is readily available. When the VW is mixed with a nurse, it is not surprising (and disappointing) that one student's friends saw this as an exercise in deviance rather than a learning opportunity.

"Well what I was telling people was that I was in SL dressed up as a nurse and they thought that was hysterical and perhaps a little naughty" (Student A).

5 Discussion

A clear research outcome is that the relationship between the learner and avatar characteristics is relevant to the experience of learning. This aligns with existing literature, which supports the notion that users form complex and varied relationships with their avatars. Projective identity theory explains this phenomenon and asserts that an avatar is either a representation of the user (with some modifications) or is a projection, aimed at controlling the perceptions of other people [28]. In essence, these are avatar creations that represent the actual-self (albeit modified) or the ideal-self [26].

Overall, these findings are in accordance with those reported in the wider literature in that the participants in this research viewed their avatars from many perspectives. Some had a type of maternal relationship with their avatar, or similarly, perceived their avatar in a doll-like way; as something to be dressed-up and played with [29]. Others saw it as an entity that represented themselves and had a strong psychological association to it [30] and others still, saw their avatar as a representation of an idealised or entirely different self [26].

Student and academic participants in this research were all required to create their own avatar. The only restriction placed on the characteristics of the build was that the avatar had to take human form. Interestingly, all academic participants, whether they created an avatar that represented their actual or ideal–self, customized their avatars in an image recognisably associated with their lecturing profession. All avatars were attired in professional business wear, for example, although they vacillated between real-self and ideal-self, adding features such as larger breasts and increased muscle tone.

Students however, demonstrated a broader range of avatar embodiment. For example, some students spoke about 'dressing up' their avatar to be what they wanted them to be or created an obvious representation of their real self. One student demonstrated what Triberti et al. [28] would describe as a clear example of impression management, when they customised their avatar to possess the physical features that they did not. This virtual veil extended to their choice of clothing and ultimately the influenced personal characteristics of the user themselves.

The modification of personal demeanour and behaviour in line with one's avatar characteristics, whilst new to nurse education research, has been extensively researched in the field of gaming. Interestingly, in previous research conducted by Hobart [31], students (a random sample from across a large mid-Western University) who created ideal-self avatars demonstrated greater learning outcomes. This was associated with higher levels of involvement, disinhibition and enjoyment than their peers who developed real-self avatars. Some of the participants during this research too, were noted to have a richer involvement when they chose to be represented by an ideal-self avatar, (such as the example previously described) however comparative learning outcomes were not measured.

Of note also, some of the participants in research became so immersed that there was almost no disconnection between the self and the avatar while in the VW. Indeed, the research demonstrated immersion to a point where the technology became inconspicuous and unobtrusive and "the virtuality of self [had] become unnoticed" [27 p. 121].

This research yielded many examples of this phenomenon. One student, who appeared withdrawn and reticent in the real-life classroom, had much more bravado and engagement as their ideal-self avatar. Another student demonstrated a high level of affective engagement in the VW when they became genuinely alarmed when their *virtual* patient was suffering.

Interestingly, students and academics alike experienced being so seamlessly subsumed into the SL experience that there was a blurring between the avatars' behaviours and real-world responses from their creators. For example, when one academic's avatar was inadvertently naked in front of a group of other avatars, the academic expressed feelings of embarrassment (in the real-world).

6   Conclusion

This research has taken place at a time where technology is disrupting nursing education practice. It is timely then that the findings of this research inform an understanding of the nature of learning the skills of nursing with students who have the opportunity to learn in a VW. These findings highlight, not just that learning can be achieved in SL, but that learning can be positively influenced by certain characteristic-capabilities of the avatar. Indeed, ideal-self avatar learners demonstrated increased enjoyment and greater engagement with the course content. Furthermore, it is apparent that the artificial, intangible world of the SL learning matrix was perceived by the participants in this research to be intensely real. Their connectedness in SL; to those within it and to themselves, are examples of the multiple knowledge networks enabled by this digital platform. So much so, that it was possible to become immersed and demonstrate real-world reactions and actions, to a simulated clinical proposition.

Further research should explore the learning outcomes of nursing students relative to the self-creation of their avatars. This would extend the existing education literature where the actualisation of an avatar is associated with intrinsic motivation and the development of self-determination. Now, presents an exciting opportunity to infuse active educational practices such as simulations in SL, to challenge existing and longstanding pedagogical practices that have less meaning as contemporary in this technological driven context of health and education.

References

1. Yoder, S., Terhorst, I.: "Beam me up, Scotty": designing the future of nursing professional development. J. Contin. Educ. Nurs. **43**(10), 456–462 (2012)
2. Gregory, S., Lee, M., Dalgarno, B., Tynan, B. (eds.): Learning in Virtual Worlds. AU Press, Athbasca Univeristy (2016)
3. Dalgarno, B., Lee, M., Carlson, L., Gregory, S., Tynan, B.: An Australian and New Zealand scoping study on the use of 3D immersive virtual worlds in higher education. Australas. J. Educ. Technol. **27**(1), 1–15 (2011)
4. Chau, M., et al.: Using 3D virtual environments to facilitate students in constructivist learning. Dec. Support Syst. **56**, 115–121 (2013)
5. Eyikara, E., Baykara, Z.: The importance of simulation in nursing education. World J. Educ. Technol. Curr. Issues **9**(1), 2–7 (2017)
6. Irwin, P., Coutts, R.: A systematic review of the experience of using second life in the education of undergraduate nurses. J. Nurs. Educ. **54**(10), 572–577 (2015)
7. Carroll, N., Richardson, I., Maolney, M., O'Reilly, P.: Working in Partnership Programme (WiPP) (2017)
8. Gore, T., Thomson, W.: Use of Simulation in undergraduate and graduate dducation. AACN Adv. Crit. Care **27**(1), 86–95 (2016)
9. Johnson, L., Adams Becker, S., Cummins, M., Estrada, V., Freeman, A., Hall, C.: NMC Horizon Report: 2016 Higher Education Edition (2016)
10. Gregory, S., et al. (eds.): Virtual worlds in Australian and New Zealand higher education: remembering the past, understanding the present and imagining the future. In: Electric Dreams: Proceedings Ascilitie, Sydney (2013)
11. Gregory, S., Jacka, L., Hillier, M., Grant, S.: Using virtual worlds in rural and regional educational institutions. Aust. Int. J. Rural Educ. **25**(2), 73–90 (2015)
12. De Gagne, J., Oh, J., Kang, J., Vorderstrasse, A., Johnson, C.: Virtual worlds in nursing education: a synthesis of the literature. J. Nurs. Educ. **52**(7), 391–400 (2013)
13. Hart, S.: Today's learners and educators: bridging the generational gaps. Teach. Learn. Nurs. **12**(4), 253–257 (2017)
14. Bell, F.: Connectivism: its place in theory-informed research and innovation in technology-enabled learning. Int. Rev. Res. Open Distance Learn. **12**(3), 98–118 (2011)
15. Clarà, M., Barberà, E.: Learning online: massive open online courses (MOOCs), connectivism, and cultural psychology. Distance Educ. **34**(1), 129–136 (2013)
16. Siemens, G.: Connectivism: a learning theory for the digital age 2005. http://www.ingedewaard.net/papers/connectivism/2005_siemens_ALearningTheoryForTheDigitalAge.pdf
17. Dunaway, M.: Connectivism: learning theory and pedagogical practice for networked information landscapes. Ref. Serv. Rev. **39**(4), 675–685 (2011)
18. Boitshwarelo, B.: Proposing an integrated research framework for connectivism: utilising theoretical synergies. Int. Rev. Res. Open Distance Learn. **12**(3), 161–179 (2011)
19. Kop, R.: The challenges to connectivist learning on open online networks: learning experiences during a massive open online course. Int. Rev. Res. Open Distance Learn. **12**(3), 19–37 (2011)
20. Bulu, S.: Place presence, social presence, co-presence, and satisfaction in virtual worlds. Comput. Educ. **58**(1), 154–161 (2012)
21. Tirado Morueta, R., Maraver López, P., Hernando Gómez, Á., Harris, V.: Exploring social and cognitive presences in communities of inquiry to perform higher cognitive tasks. Internet Higher Educ. **31**, 122–131 (2016)

22. Yang, J., Quadir, B., Chen, N.-S., Miao, Q.: Effects of online presence on learning performance in a blog-based online course. Internet Higher Educ **30**(Supplement C), 11–20 (2016)

23. Zhan, Z., Mei, H.: Academic self-concept and social presence in face-to-face and online learning: perceptions and effects on students' learning achievement and satisfaction across environments. Comput. Educ. **69**(Supplement C), 131–138 (2013)

24. Corbin, J., Strauss, A.: Grounded theory research: procedures, canons, and evaluative criteria. Qual. Sociol. **13**(1), 3–21 (1990)

25. Polit, D., Beck, C.: Essentials of nursing research. Appraising evidence for nursing practice. 8 ed. Wolters Kluwer. Lippincott Williams and Wilkins, Sydney (2014)

26. Mancini, T., Sibilla, F.: Offline personality and avatar customisation. Discrepancy profiles and avatar identification in a sample of MMORPG players. Comput. Hum. Behav. **69** (Supplement C), 275–283 (2017)

27. Seo, Y., Kim, M., Jung, Y., Lee, D.: Avatar face recognition and self-presence. Comput. Hum. Behav. **69**(Supplement C), 120–127 (2017)

28. Triberti, S., Durosini, I., Aschieri, F., Villani, D., Riva, G.: Changing avatars, changing selves? The influence of social and contextual expectations on digital rendition of identity. CyberPsychol. Behav. Soc. Networking **20**(8), 501–507 (2017)

29. Liao, C.: Virtual fashion play as embodied identity re/assembling: second life fashion bloggers and their avatar bodies. In: Peachey, A., Childs, M. (eds.) Reinventing Ourselves: Contemporary Concepts of Identity in Virtual Worlds. Springer Series in Immersive Environments. Springer, London (2011). https://doi.org/10.1007/978-0-85729-361-9_6

30. Bessière, K., Seay, A., Kiesler, S.: The ideal elf: identity exploration in World of Warcraft. CyberPsychol. Behav. **10**(4), 530–535 (2007)

31. Hobart, M.: Learning from myself. Avatars and educational video games. Current Issues in Education **5**(3), 1–15 (2012)

Escaping into a Simulated Environment: A Preliminary Investigation into How MMORPGs Are Used to Cope with Real Life Stressors

Lorelle Bowditch[1]([✉])(iD), Anjum Naweed[1](iD), and Janine Chapman[2](iD)

[1] Appleton Institute of Behavioural Science, Central Queensland University, Wayville, Australia
l.bowditch@cqu.edu.au
[2] National Centre for Education and Training on Addiction (NCETA), Flinders University, Adelaide, Australia

Abstract. The mechanisms underlying Internet Gaming Disorder (IGD) are complex, and in order to gain a better understanding of the pathways to IGD a broader investigation of the social context and life environment of gamers is important. Little is understood about the real-life experiences of gamers who use internet gaming for relief from real-life problems. This study aimed to explore the types of external stressors internet gamers experience, and the ways in which internet gaming is used to cope with these stressors. As part of a larger psychosocial survey, adult World of Warcraft (WoW) players (N = 217) were asked for comments about a stressful event. Of this sample, 46 participants mentioned WoW in their response. Content analysis was used to analyse key themes relating to external stressors that led players to engage in WoW gameplay. Key themes of real-life stress; health issues; financial problems; and, family and social problems emerged. These findings showed the variety of external stressors that can lead an individual to be motivated to escape through MMORPG play. This study adds to our understanding of the relationship between gamers and video games, specifically in times of stress. Future investigation should examine links to gaming outcomes.

Keywords: Internet Gaming Disorder · Escapism · Coping

1 Introduction

In the internet gaming context, escapism involves "playing to relax or escape from real life or avoid real life problems" [1]. Being motivated to play internet games for escapist reasons is a key predictor of the negative outcomes associated with internet gaming [2–6]. In response to this association, escapism has been included as a proposed diagnostic criteria for Internet Gaming Disorder (IGD) in the most recent edition of the *Diagnostic and Statistical Manual of Mental Disorders* (DSM-5) [1]. The inclusion of IGD as an

© Springer Nature Singapore Pte Ltd. 2019
A. Naweed et al. (Eds.): ASC 2019, CCIS 1067, pp. 46–57, 2019.
https://doi.org/10.1007/978-981-32-9582-7_4

emerging diagnosis has led to an influx of interest into isolating individual factors that can predict IGD [7].

Massively Multiplayer Online Role-Playing Games (MMORPGs) are one genre of internet game implicated in the attribution of behaviors associated with IGD. Excessive engagement in MMORPGs can lead to some players becoming compulsively preoc-cupied with the game at the exclusion of psychosocial needs and interests [5, 8, 9]. World of Warcraft (WoW) is a popular example of an MMORPG. WoW takes place in a fantasy 3D virtual world in which players create avatars to interact in real-time with the environment and other players in order to explore, fight, complete objectives and gain rewards. Players can join or form social groups known as 'guilds', play against non-playable characters (Player vs Environment), other players (Player vs Player) or role-play. Group objectives can be completed by forming a group with friends or by using an in-game grouping tool [10].

1.1 Escape and Engagement and Internet Gaming

Established research indicates that mental illness (e.g. depression and anxiety), lone-liness, boredom, lack of satisfaction and success in life are all linked to gaming problems [11, 12]. Excessive engagement is associated with heightened impulsivity traits, inhibitory deficits [13], and structural deficits in areas of the brain involved in the cognitive process of decision-making [14]. However, a clearer distinction between high engagement and problematic engagement in internet gaming is arguably required in order to avoid confusing passion with disorder, and ultimately pathologizing healthy gamers [15].

Current work proposes that problematic internet gameplay could be reframed as a stress response [12]. Problematic real-life situations can lead an individual to engage in online gaming in order to alleviate dysphoric moods or fulfil unmet needs [16], as well as to manage, minimize and escape stress [12]. From this perspective, escapist gameplay may reflect a coping strategy to deal with real-life stress, rather than evidence of IGD per se [7, 17]. For example, Kardefelt-Winther [16] found that the risk of negative outcomes associated with internet gaming is higher in players with pre-existing psychosocial problems such as stress and lower self-esteem.

However, more recent research suggests that individual differences in the type of coping style employed in times of stress may be a key factor in whether gameplay results in negative outcomes. Bowditch et al. [3] found that having an engaged, problem focused coping style was a key moderator in the relationship between escapism and IGD-related outcomes (e.g. withdrawal, preoccupation). These types of coping strategies, including problem solving and cognitive restructuring, seemed to play a protective role in reducing potential harms, suggesting that for some people, gameplaying as a response to stress could be adaptive rather than maladaptive [3].

1.2 Aim of the Current Study

From this overview it is clear that the mechanisms underlying problematic gaming are complex and would benefit from a much broader investigation of the social context and life environment of the individual [18]. Research on this area is still in its infancy, and little is known about the real-life experiences of gamers who use internet gaming for relief from real-life problems. The aim of the current study is to explore the types of external stressors internet gamers experience, and the ways in which internet gaming is used to cope with these stressors. This investigation is exploratory in nature, using qualitative data collected from a sample of WoW players. The study will provide preliminary insight into the range of internal and external factors that might lead an individual to escape and engage in internet gameplay in order to cope, and in-turn add to the understanding of the pathways to IGD.

2 Methods

2.1 Participants and Procedure

Respondents were selected following their participation in a larger cross-sectional survey of adult WoW players [3]. An invitation to complete the larger survey was posted on mainstream outlets (gaming forums, Facebook). All participants were over 18 years of age and current subscribers and players of World of Warcraft.

The original survey was anonymous with no identifiable data collected and gained the approval of the University's Human Research Ethics Committee (Approval No. *H17/05-91*). Qualitative data was gathered as part of Tobin's [19] Coping Strategies Inventory (CSI), which was included as the final section of the original online survey. Survey participants were asked to imagine a stressful event that occurred in their life. A textbox was provided that allowed (but did not require) participants to describe the stressful event. Participants were also given the opportunity to comment at the end of the survey regarding any issues that had been raised in the survey. A total of 117 participants left a comment in the first textbox. In total, 26 comments were left in the textbox at the end of the survey, 19 of these comments were from participants who had commented earlier. The current sample is based on the $n = 46$ participants who wrote open-ended responses based on playing WoW as a way to relieve stress.

Demographic variables are shown in Table 1. Of the 46 respondents, most were female (83%). Respondents' age ranged from 18 to 74 years ($M = 36$; $SD = 11$). While based in Australia, the international reach of study recruitment meant most participants indicated they were born in the USA (63%). The majority of the sample were educated to college or university level (75%), in paid employment (61%), were married or in a domestic partnership (71%) and just over half (57%) of the sample were part of a couple, half of whom had at least 1 child.

2.2 Data Analysis

Qualitative analysis is a common method used in research involving internet use [20–22]. Preliminary data was analyzed thematically using an inductive approach [23] in a 4-stage process: (1) comments from the first textbox were read in-depth and responses from each participant that mentioned WoW were kept for further analysis; (2) if the same participant mentioned WoW in the second textbox, this comment was added to the first (62 individual comments from 46 participants); (3) initial coding

Table 1. Characteristics of participants who mentioned WoW in their response

Variable	% (n)
Gender	
Male	17 (8)
Female	83 (38)
Birthplace	
Canada	17(8)
Europe	7 (3)
New Zealand	2 (1)
South America	2 (1)
Africa	2 (1)
United Kingdom	7 (3)
United States of America	63 (29)
Education	
Primary school	7 (3)
Secondary school	18 (8)
College/TAFE/Diploma	38 (17)
University degree	31 (14)
Postgraduate degree	7 (3)
Relationship status	
Single, never married	5 (1)
Married or domestic partnership	71 (15)
Divorced/Separated	24 (5)
Household description	
Lone person	13 (6)
Couple without children	28 (13)
One parent family	15 (7)
Couple with child(ren)	28 (13)
Other	15 (7)
Paid Work Status	
In paid work	61 (28)
Not in paid work	39 (18)

using qualitative analysis software NVivo (ver. 12) identified broad themes relating to external stressors that led players to engage in WoW gameplay; and finally (4) axial coding identified the properties of key themes and the relationships amongst them. Both initial and axial coding were minimally refined due to the preliminary nature of the analysis, thus limiting the extent to which themes relating to gaming outcomes and coping were analysed.

3   Results

3.1   Sample Characteristics

Table 2 shows the game-play style of the respondents. Almost all respondents were members of a guild (93%) and predominately played Player versus Environment (PvE) (85%). The majority of respondents completed objectives that required group-play with people that they knew (52%).

Table 2. Game-play style of participants

Play style variable	% (n)
Member of a Guild	
Yes	93 (42)
No	7 (3)
Type of Gameplay	
Player vs Environment	85 (39)
Player vs Player	9 (4)
Role-Play	4 (2)
Unsure	2 (1)
Type of Group Play	
People I know	52 (24)
Premade group tool	39 (18)
Don't play in a group	9 (4)

3.2   Key Themes

Four key themes relating to external stressors that led individuals to interact with WoW were identified. These were: (1) Real-Life Stress; (2) Health Issues; (3) Financial Problems; and (4) Family and Social Problems. Sub-themes relating to each of these are reconstructed and discussed in more detail in the following sections with a summary and frequency of statements relating to each theme and sub-theme shown in Table 3. Excerpts from the data are taken to support and illustrate points where relevant. Identification tags are assigned to each of the 46 participants in the order in which their responses were recorded in the larger survey.

Real-Life Stress. Real-life stress was a significant theme identified by respondents as an external stressor that led them to interact with WoW. This theme was divided into sub-themes of work stress, stress from study and life events.

Work Stress. Work stress was a type of real-life stressor of concern, for example:

> "[After a] bad day at work [that was] very busy and stressful, [I] use WoW to relax and unwind" [p_49].

> "[I am] working as an educator and only have time to play on Friday's and Saturday's. Life is stressful, but wow is fun" [p_74].

Table 3. Summary of preliminary thematic analysis.

Themes	Sub-themes	Frequency of statements (%)	Theme totals
Real-life stress	Work stress	5 (36%)	14 (22.5%)
	Stress from study	5 (36%)	
	Life events	4 (28%)	
Health issues	Physical health issues	10 (59%)	17 (27.5%)
	Mental health issues	7 (41%)	
Financial problems	Loss of employment/unemployment	5 (50%)	10 (16%)
	Money problems/Poverty	5 (50%)	
Family and social problems	Relationship with significant other	4 (19%)	21 (34%)
	Abuse	2 (10%)	
	Caring/Health of a loved one	6 (28%)	
	Loneliness	2 (10%)	
	Bereavement	3 (14%)	
	Family dynamics	1 (5%)	
	Socializing/Social skills	3 (14%)	

Stress from Study. The sub-theme of stress from study emerged, with respondents indicating that they used WoW to relax or have a *"break"* from their studies.

"I started to play WoW while writing my master's thesis. It was a good break from the real life…" [p_74].

However, potentially problematic WoW engagement was also noted:

"I started playing WoW during my PhD to escape the daily hell that my life had become. Combined with near daily use of alcohol, it let me escape and survive the most dark time in my life" [p_325].

Life Events. Non-specific life events were mentioned as sub-themes of real-life stress that respondents identified as external stressors that led them to interact with WoW as a distraction and a way to relax:

"When dealing with stressful events, I usually want time to sort through all of my choices, I like to give myself time to consider the pros and cons. Since this does take some time, I will occasionally play video games (including WoW) as a way to relax and give me something else to think about for a bit" [p_24].

Health Issues. The effect of health issues led respondents to engage with WoW. Statements mentioned playing WoW to *"distract"* themselves from their illness, and as a tool they used to interact with friends online when they were housebound. Health issues were divided into sub-themes of physical and mental health issues.

Physical Health Issues. Respondents mentioned a range of physical health issues that lead them to play WoW for distraction or to relieve boredom, for example:

"...I play WoW frequently in the morning hours to distract from my GI [gastro intestinal] issues, and to calm myself and try to keep a low heart rate where I have dysautonomia[1]" [p_79].

"WoW made chemo tolerable" [p_71].

"I played when my spine was severed, and I could not walk around that's how I started. I was bored of just sitting there" [p_148].

Mental Health Issues. Respondents engaged with WoW to relieve symptoms of their mental illness, or to aid in their recovery from mental illness:

"Usually I play [WoW] for anxiety relief" [p_29].

"I was depressed and suicidal and ended up checking myself into a [psychiatric] ward to try and get some help. When I got out, I found that putting myself into a busy schedule between work, WoW, and a few friends really helped, and ended up motivating me to join a top 200 guild[2] in WoW" [p_104].

Financial Problems. Some respondents mentioned that they engaged with WoW in order to distract them from financial issues that had experienced from loss or lack of employment and budget problems/poverty.

Loss of Employment/Unemployment. Respondents engaged with WoW to distract from their employment problems and for enjoyment:

"I have been struggling with my economy [financial situation] due to being unemployed. This has been ongoing for my whole adult life (±20 years). It's safe to say I feel better when playing WoW, than calculating pennies I don't have" [p_55].

Budget Problems/Poverty. WoW engagement was also used as a coping strategy to deal with poverty and the financial stress caused by budget problems:

"... [my husband and I] played a lot of WoW to cope with being very poor" [p_20].

"We just lost our home and had to file bankruptcy when we had health issues...so now, we play to give us time to not think" [p_91].

Family and Social Problems. Issues associated with family and relationships were the most represented within the data. Statements mentioned issues associated with the family and socializing/social skills.

---

[1] Disorder of the autonomic nervous system.

[2] Highly ranked guild in terms of in-game objective completion.

Relationship with Significant Other. It was noted that WoW was used not only as a tool to cope with external stressors, but also as a way of developing relationships and building friendships:

> "My husband was having an emotional affair with another woman while I was in the middle of an episode of depression, we had been drifting apart due to opposite schedules and it was hard on me, we used to spend a lot of time together, playing WoW was one of the things that brought us closer in the past. We are trying to work through this and doing things together like we used to do is top priority according to our therapist. He suggested we play together more often" [p_10].

Abuse. WoW engagement was used to *"escape"* from different kinds of abuse from others at home and in the family:

> "My mother was physically and emotionally abusive, I was living with her [when] WoW [was] first released and as I got sucked more in to it. [WoW] was my escape, literally and figuratively" [p_20].

Caring/Health of a Loved One. The majority of the key theme 'family and social problems' involved respondents reflecting on how WoW had helped them to cope with issues that related to caring for family members that were unwell:

> "My mum is a terminal cancer patient, and I stay at home to care for her. [...] I often play WoW on silent on my laptop when my mum falls asleep, so I don't disturb her. It's my place to escape, where I can 'heal'[3] whatever ails my friends..." [p_99].

> "My daughter is staying with me right now and she has some mental [health] issues. I'm helping her deal with them as best I can until she can get professional help. She moved here from another state and needs to wait for her insurance to start up. It is extremely stressful. Despite the problem with my daughter, I still manage to get my WoW time in. It gives me solace and escape" [p_193].

Loneliness. Engagement with WoW was also used as a tool to cope with loneliness and connect socially:

> "[I] moved to a new city (for work). [I] had no friends. [It was] hard to make friends in the city. [I] got kinda depressed. [I] asked old friends if they wanted to play WoW with me again. They agreed! (7 of them). [It] really helped my daily mood and outlook knowing I had friends to hang out [with online] when I got home from work" [p_126].

Bereavement. WoW was used to cope with bereavement. Respondents mentioned that although they did not engage with WoW immediately, eventually WoW gameplay became a way of *"helping"* or *"rewarding"* themselves. One respondent however reflected that WoW engagement may have been at the expense of engagement with education:

> "My best friend died suddenly. I spent time away from WoW at first, but ultimately used it to reward myself. Instead of doing homework while in nursing school, I played WoW before bed for a time after her death. I still passed nursing school though" [p_114].

---

[3] A reference to in-game abilities.

Family Dynamics. One respondent reflected on using WoW to cope with the stress from seeing family members for the first time in years:

> "Planning a wedding with family that lives many states away. It was stressful because some family members I haven't seen in years…I play WoW to destress. It's calming to systematically complete quests and hunt AP[4]" [p_135].

Socializing/Social Skills. Respondents stated that they used WoW as a social outlet, and to develop social skills:

> "In my perspective WoW has helped me perform better at work by helping me learn some acceptable social skills" [p_137].

> "I've never been a social girl, so gaming is what soothe[s] me the most" [p_15].

> "[After having cut back on WoW time due to problematic use and issues with mental health] … I still tend to be a shut-in and feel more comfortable with online interactions" [p_165].

4   Discussion

This exploratory investigation summarizes the variety of external stressors and internal emotional states that lead individuals to engage in WoW gameplay. The term *"escape"* was used often during responses for every key theme. Escapism, as aforementioned, is frequently linked to IGD-related symptomology. However recent research has also found that escapism is not always negative, and has the potential to be adaptive in some circumstances [3]. The current analyses further support this notion.

Most references to external stressors were associated with family and social problems, specifically around caring for loved ones who were suffering from ill-health. In 2015, it was estimated that 39.8 million adults in the United States had provided unpaid care to another adult in the 12 months prior. One in five of the caregivers reported a high level of physical strain, and two in five considered their situation as emotionally stressful [24]. With reference to WoW engagement providing *"escape"*, *"solace"* and the ability to *"heal"* their friends, gameplay seemed to provide a space that allowed caregivers to increase their positive feelings and alleviate negative moods.

A desire to socialize and develop social skills emerged as a motivator for respondents to engage in WoW gameplay. The majority of respondents stated that they were part of a guild and played with people they knew. This idea reflects the outcomes of previous research in which players of MMORPGs stated that the social aspects of this type of game had the biggest appeal [25]. In seminal work, Yee [2] found that 39.4% of male respondents and 53.3% of female respondents considered the friendships formed while playing an MMORPG were comparable or better than their 'real-world' friends. Communication channels that exist in MMORPGs allow players to: (1) optimize their self-presentation; (2) reallocate cognitive resources that are usually used to maintain acceptable forms of non-verbal gestures towards the structure

---

[4] Achievement Points are a scoring system awarded for completing game objectives.

and content of the verbal message itself; and (3) send, and then receive personal and intimate messages in return. This leads to interactions that become more intimate and positive [2].

Statements related to physical health issues were the most salient. Respondents who mentioned physical health issues predominately suffered from chronic conditions, with some stating that they suffered from extremely serious, life threatening ailments. Respondents found their engagement with WoW gave them *"support"*, *"escape"*, *"time to think"*, a *"distraction"*, a way to make their condition *"tolerable"* and as a *"way to pass time"*. The use of Virtual Reality (VR) has been used as an effective method of reducing pain in patients with chronic pain. It was found that VR was effective in engaging patients, and thus distracting them from their pain [26]. Immersion in VR was also found to impact patients physiologically, by lowering heart rates, respiration rates, skin temperature and skin resistance, leading to a relaxing effect [27]. Although these studies involve a VR program specifically designed for the purpose of distraction and relaxation, WoW includes features that promote immersion [2], and when coupled with a system of social support, chronically ill patients may find relief from the pain and isolation associated with their illness.

Stress brought on by real-life situations, specifically work and study-related stress, was an important factor that led respondents to engage in WoW gameplay. Although one respondent mentioned that WoW gameplay during stressful study times negatively impacted their results, most cited positive consequences to their gameplay, such that WoW gave them a *"break"*, *"escape"*, and a chance to *"go over"* study material in their head. Respondents also stated that WoW gave them a chance to *"relax"* after a stressful day at work.

Surprisingly, financial problems emerged as a stressor that promotes WoW engagement. WoW is often considered one of the more expensive MMORPGs to play, due to the its monthly subscription-based model. However, a monthly subscription to WoW costs US \$14.99 ($\sim$ AU \$21.50) which is comparable to other forms of entertainment such as the price of one cinema ticket or a Netflix subscription [28–30].

4.1 Limitations and Future Research

Due to the preliminary nature of this exploratory study, there are limitations to this research. Gaming outcomes were not included in the current analyses therefore it remains unknown whether the coping strategies used by the sample were associated with objectively negative or positive effects. There is potential in future articles to extend this preliminary study to include outcomes in the analyses.

In addition, the sample was skewed toward female respondents. Although this is a limiting factor in terms of being representative of the general population of internet gamers, who are predominately male, it is important to recognize that the population of female gamers is increasing yet research to date has predominately focused on male gamers due to the sampling methods used [3].

5 Conclusions

In conclusion, this research plays an important role in investigating the different types of external stressors that lead individuals to escape and engage in MMORPG gameplay, and the ways in which WoW is used to deal with real life stressful experiences. Although preliminary, it aids in the understanding of the ways in which internet game players cope with stress in their daily life; gives useful insight into the ways in which escaping daily stressors through WoW may benefit rather than harm players and informs future research into the multifaceted pathways to IGD.

References

1. American Psychiatric Association. Diagnostic and statistical manual of mental disorders: DSM-5, American Psychological Society, Washington, DC (2013)
2. Yee, N.: The psychology of massively multi-user online role-playing games: motivations, emotional investment, relationships and problematic usage. In: Schroeder, R., Axelsson, A. S. (eds.) Avatars at Work and Play. CSCW, vol. 34, pp. 187–207. Springer, Dordrecht (2006). https://doi.org/10.1007/1-4020-3898-4_9
3. Bowditch, L., Chapman, J., Naweed, A.: Do coping strategies moderate the relationship between escapism and negative gaming outcomes in World of Warcraft (MMORPG) players? Comput. Hum. Behav. **86**, 69–76 (2018)
4. Billieux, J., et al.: Why do you play world of warcraft? An in-depth exploration of self-reported motivations to play online and in-game behaviours in the virtual world of Azeroth. Comput. Hum. Behav. **29**(1), 103–109 (2013)
5. Kaczmarek, L.D., Drążkowski, D.: MMORPG escapism predicts decreased well-being: examination of gaming time, game realism beliefs, and online social support for offline problems. Cyberpsychol. Behav. Soc. Networking **17**(5), 298–302 (2014)
6. Kahn, A.S., et al.: The trojan player typology: a cross-genre, cross-cultural, behaviorally validated scale of video game play motivations. Comput. Hum. Behav. **49**, 354–361 (2015)
7. Kardefelt-Winther, D.: Conceptualizing internet use disorders: addiction or coping process? Psychiatry Clin. Neurosci. **71**(7), 459–466 (2017)
8. Hagström, D., Kaldo, V.: Escapism among players of MMORPGs—conceptual clarification, its relation to mental health factors, and development of a new measure. Cyberpsychol. Behav. Soc. Networking **17**(1), 19–25 (2014)
9. Kuss, D.J., Louws, J., Wiers, R.W.: Online gaming addiction? Motives predict addictive play behavior in massively multiplayer online role-playing games. Cyberpsychol. Behav. Soc. Networking **15**(9), 480–485 (2012)
10. Blizzard Entertainment. World of Warcraft: New players guide. 2019. https://worldofwarcraft.com/en-gb/game/new-playersguide
11. Myrseth, H., et al.: Predictors of gaming behavior among military peacekeepers – exploring the role of boredom and loneliness in relation to gaming problems. J. Mil. Stud. **8**(1), 1–10 (2017)
12. Snodgrass, J.G., et al.: A vacation from your mind: problematic online gaming is a stress response. Comput. Hum. Behav. **38**, 248–260 (2014)
13. Deleuze, J., et al.: Established risk factors for addiction fail to discriminate between healthy gamers and gamers endorsing DSM-5 Internet gaming disorder. J. Behav. Addict. **6**(4), 516–524 (2017)

14. Zhou, F., et al.: Orbitofrontal gray matter deficits as marker of Internet gaming disorder: converging evidence from a cross-sectional and prospective longitudinal design. Addict. Biol. **24**(1), 100–109 (2019)
15. Deleuze, J., et al.: Passion or addiction? Correlates of healthy versus problematic use of videogames in a sample of French-speaking regular players. Addict. Behav. **82**, 114–121 (2018)
16. Kardefelt-Winther, D.: Problematizing excessive online gaming and its psychological predictors. Comput. Hum. Behav. **31**, 118–122 (2014)
17. Griffiths, M.D., et al.: Working towards an international consensus on criteria for assessing internet gaming disorder: a critical commentary on Petry, et al. Addiction **111**(1), 167–175 (2016)
18. Deleuze, J., et al.: Escaping reality through videogames is linked to an implicit preference for virtual over real-life stimuli. J. Affect. Disord. **245**, 1024–1031 (2019)
19. Tobin, D., et al.: The hierachical factor structure of the coping strategies inventory. Cogn. Ther. Res. **13**(4), 343–361 (1989)
20. Irwin, S.V., Naweed, A.: BM'ing, Throwing, Bug Exploiting, and Other Forms of (Un) Sportsmanlike Behavior in CS:GO Esports. Games and Cult., 1–23 (2018)
21. Kim, H.S., et al.: From the mouths of social media users: a focus group study exploring the social casino gaming-online gambling link. J. Behav. Addict. **5**(1), 115–121 (2016)
22. Symons, K., et al.: A qualitative study into parental mediation of adolescents' internet use. Comput. Hum. Behav. **73**, 423–432 (2017)
23. Saldaña, J.: The Coding Manual for Qualitative Researchers. Sage, UK (2012)
24. National Alliance for Caregiving and P.P. Institute. Caregivers in the U.S. (2015). https://www.caregiving.org/wp-content/uploads/2015/05/2015_CaregivingintheUS_Executive-Summary-June-4_WEB.pdf
25. Griffiths, M.D., Davies, M.N.O., Chappell, D.: Demographic factors and playing variables in online computer gaming. Cyberpsychol. Behav. **7**(4), 479–487 (2004)
26. Wiederhold, B.K., et al.: Virtual reality as a distraction technique in chronic pain patients. Cyberpsychol. Behav. Soc. Networking **17**(6), 346–352 (2014)
27. Wiederhold, B.K., Davis, R., Wiederhold, M.D.: The effects of immersiveness on physiology. In: Virtual Environments in Clinical Psychology and Neuroscience: Methods and Techniques in Advanced Patient–Therapist Interaction, pp. 52–60, IOS Press, Amsterdam (1998)
28. World of Warcraft no longer requires a game purchase, just a subscription (2018). https://www.polygon.com/2018/7/17/17583338/world-of-warcraft-legion-battle-chest-subscription-only. Accessed 17 Jul 2018
29. Shoard, C.: US cinema ticket prices reach record high, @guardian (2016)
30. BBCWorld, Netflix raises prices for US customers (2019). https://www.bbc.com/news/business-46881977

Design and Application

Disrupting the Familiar: Applying Educational Theories to Simulation-Based Learning and Assessment Design

Irwyn Shepherd[1(✉)], Elyssebeth Leigh[2], and Amanda Davies[3]

[1] Monash University, Melbourne, VIC 3168, Australia
irwyn.shepherd@monash.edu
[2] University of Technology, Sydney, NSW 2007, Australia
Elyssebeth.leigh@icloud.com
[3] Rabdan Academy, Abu Dhabi, UAE
adavies@ra.ac.ae

Abstract. As a practice-oriented, experience-based approach to education, simulation is sometimes accused of lacking educational theory, and susceptible to questions about validity. Lewin [1] asserts that 'there is nothing so practical as good theory' and we propose, conversely in regard simulation, that 'there is nothing so theoretical as good practice'. We introduce the ADELIS© model for learning design, to illustrate a means for disrupting the 'theory versus practice' debate by focusing attention on how to demonstrate that sound educational theory underlies simulation practice. The ADELIS© model invites theorists to recognize the urgency of pragmatic needs to enact learning, and asks practitioners to engage with the value and validity of using a researcher's 'long view' to examine and improve learning outcomes. The recurring inability of theory and practice to bridge the gap between them is a 'wicked' problem [2], and as such is in the Cynefin Domain of 'Complex' knowledge [3]. Addressing such problems involves unique responses for specific contexts, paying attention to what is required for effective working in this Domain develops a capacity for handling uncertainty and managing complexity familiar terrain for education designers. Successful use of simulation in learning contexts occurs even when there is no obvious link between practice and theories of learning [4]. Using the ADELIS© model for learning design supports theoretically well-formed good practice in simulation design and application. Outcomes include effective learning programs, well informed applications of theory to practice, and assessment strategies enabling educators to track the results well beyond immediate learning experiences [5]. This paper uses cases to demonstrate how theory and practice can collaborate, with positive impacts on educational design.

Keywords: Theories of education · Theory versus practice · Simulation

1 Introduction

Simulation is a practice-oriented, experience-based approach to knowledge and skill acquisition, sometimes accused of lacking educational theory [7] and susceptible to questions about validity [8]. A vital step in discovering why this occurs and provide

© Springer Nature Singapore Pte Ltd. 2019
A. Naweed et al. (Eds.): ASC 2019, CCIS 1067, pp. 61–76, 2019.
https://doi.org/10.1007/978-981-32-9582-7_5

education-based solutions to help mitigate areas of contention, requires identifying differing stakeholder perspectives.

This paper identifies, and clusters, individuals working in the field of simulation into three groups based on their orientation towards five key factors. The first group are called 'Practitioners' who are highly pragmatic, focusing on practicalities of how to get on with the job. The second group are 'Researchers' having a theoretical perspective on analysing work, and the third group are 'Practitioner-Researchers' who have a foot in each of the other two worlds, appreciating the urgency of the practicalities while also seeking to understand the 'why' explaining how the process has an impact on learning [6].

2   Context

Why is it important for simulation specialists to know about, and understand the implications of their own - and others' - orientations to getting work done? Why would such knowledge be relevant to the collaborative processes involved in designing, building and using simulations and simulators? In the context of using simulation as a method for facilitating learning, five key factors are particularly important in helping individuals attend to achieving specific work results. These identify that members of each group - when asked - demonstrate a primary focus that is distinctively related to how they consider their work, what is expected of them, how specific tasks should be completed and particular goals are to be achieved. Table 1 lists the factors and briefly notes the respective attitudes of members of each cluster.

The five factors are as follows: (1) a primary orientation to work tasks on a continuum from 'doing' to 'theorising'; (2) factors that pique curiosity, ranging from pragmatic solutions for completing tasks to needing to understand why and how things operate in specific conditions; (3) concerns the kind of questions asked in regard to completion of tasks versus generation of new knowledge and understanding; (4) is particularly important in the field of simulation as it concerns the verifiability/validity - or otherwise - of specific practices and claims about them. "If it works - use" is a typical practitioner perspective, while researchers will ask "If it works - why and how does it do so - and will it do the same thing next time?" Finally, there is (5) the factor of time. From their pragmatic approach, Practitioners want things to happen quickly. Time is often 'against them' as they work to prepare new recruits and create 'work-ready' students nearing graduation. Conversely - for Researchers, time is simply one tool, among many, to be expended as they see fit, in the search for in-depth answers to 'wicked problems'.

Practitioner-Researchers seem to begin at one end of the continuum, or the other, and gradually migrate their thinking towards a 'centrist' perspective seeking to balance the perspectives and goals of each end of the spectrum in relation to specific tasks and work goals. At this time there is speculation that each stance feels more 'comfortable' and relevant for different people, and individuals tend to move one way or the other along the continuum as they acquire information and increase their understanding and knowledge of the world [6].

Table 1. Comparing Practitioner, Researcher and Practitioner-Researcher concerns

Feature	Practitioner	Researcher	Practitioner-Researcher
Primary orientation	Complete work tasks, achieve direct goals. Research useful if directly linked to action	Identify questions worth research; Gain insights into results of practice, new knowledge and understanding are benefits	First to practice then to research, also to achieve integration of both. Broader view than practitioner focus, more practical than 'pure' research
Curiosity	Driven by work needs, not by a 'need to know' for its own sake	Driven by 'need to know' for its own sake, less concern for practical uses	Driven by work needs **and** 'need to know' Values unified approaches to action
Questions	Seeks information about 'how to' act; unconcerned about potential for creating 'new knowledge'	Keen to generate new knowledge, less interested in possible applications of answers derived from research	Concerned to know about how to apply new knowledge, and **also** interested in, and aware of capacity to, generate it from *within* practice
Verifiability/ 'purity' of methodology	Pragmatic, not interested in verifiability. Purity of method less important than fast access and application	Primary concern is veracity of research methods/findings. Need to demonstrate methodology adheres to standards	Has pragmatic stance of practitioners in regard to usability of knowledge; knows that research can justify *unconventional* practice
Time frames	Focus on direct needs of work. Less interested in long time scales. Needs 'quick returns' on investments	Long time frames, completes complex projects, develops information about 'trends' to show general implications of research results	Needs to meet quick goals interested in researching practice for both mid-term improvements, longer term understanding and change

Tension between the knowledge sets of Practitioners and Researchers tends to extend the gap between them, rather than encouraging collaboration, thus the problem of mutual respect and understanding remains real and constant. As a 'wicked' problem [2], its resolution seems to lie within the Cynefin Domain of 'Complex' knowledge [3] where actions to address relevant problems produce uniquely contextualised responses, while allowing for development of generalisable knowledge for use by both practitioners and researchers. For example, Davies's model [5, 9] for evaluating simulation-based learning is an example of a Practitioner-Researcher perspective on the issue, providing both a means for extending evaluation beyond training environment to work contexts, and beginning to address industry issues and demands [10, 11].

Drawing on this research, and using a needs analysis approach, we identify emergent needs and scaffold related elements into a framework for designing and using simulation, uniting consideration of simulation from design to debriefing and evaluation. thus, we are modelling a way to combine 'research' and 'practice' using a rigorous, practical method and applying it to assessing simulation-based learning.

Like other learning and teaching methods, simulation-based education, requires attention to theories and models underpinning and guiding design, development, delivery and evaluation of interventions. Evidence continues to indicate that the successful use of simulation is not well matched with relevant theories of learning or application of good education practices [7] although its successes indicate the links exist and are integral to effect practice. Lack of awareness of relevant theory can cause mistakes in the design phase; and it can be ignored when answers arrive too long after questions were asked. Given that the purpose of simulation is to increase and improve learning opportunities - through use of dynamic, immersive, learner-focused processes - continuing inattention to educational underpinnings is a matter of concern. From quality control, validity and reliability perspectives, it clearly has implications for users of simulation aiming to achieve effective learning outcomes, mitigate risk and demonstrate a return on investment.

3 An Educational Approach

In light of the evidence in the literature about the education theory–simulation practice gap, we advocate for a strategic approach to mitigate its effects. From an educational perspective this means ensuring use of appropriate theory to frame design and use, followed by evaluation to confirm that participants' learning experiences in a simulation activity generate on-going learning and effective workplace applications. We introduce a model to help educators consider different educational theory perspectives and approaches [6] and provide two cases studies demonstrating application of this approach.

We introduce an educational framework (called ADELIS[1]) designed to reduce the gap between theory and practice using a multi-dimensional model for ensuring educational fidelity[2] as a fundamental prerequisite for designing authentic simulation-based teaching, learning and assessment and thus advancing capability. This framework - and its accompanying model - draws together and applies a focused spectrum of evidence-based, designed and validated educational models and tools [9].

Application of the ADELIS[©] model is underpinned by a needs analysis approach in which the authors draw on earlier work by Davies [9, 12], Shepherd [7] and others, identifying the elements required to better design, develop, deliver and evaluate a simulation activity. The goal is to ensure a simulation intervention effectively and constructively aligns learning and enhances the learning experience. By working to

---

[1] ADELIS is a composite acronym of the three developers' initials.

[2] Striving to design and deliver as precisely as can be attained, educational outcomes using appropriate education theories/frameworks, learning models and instructional design models to achieve identified learning outcomes (observable and measurable knowledge/skills/attitudes/values [7]).

close the theory-practice gap, this approach ensures simulation participants are better prepared from a cognitive, attitudinal, psychomotor and resilience perspective resulting in enhanced preparedness for future employment requirements and challenges.

4   Setting the Scene

While there is an increased awareness of the theory-practice gap [12–17] evidence continues to demonstrate that successful use of simulations in learning contexts remains insufficiently supported with relevant theories of learning or application of good education practices [7]. For example, healthcare and professional services have repeatedly identified the need for more research around the use of simulation, with experts identifying that simulation-based research needs to be grounded in theoretical and conceptual frameworks [18–22].

5   The ADELIS© Model - Five Iterative Steps for Effective Design

The ADELIS© model (Fig. 1) focuses on closing the gap between the theory and practice of simulation by enhancing the effect of both. This ensures that simulation activity achieves educational standards that (for example) reduce clinical theory-practice gaps that can impact on achieving levels of competence and safety. As noted above, the gap arises partly, from the different speeds at which theorists and practitioners engage with their respective contributions.

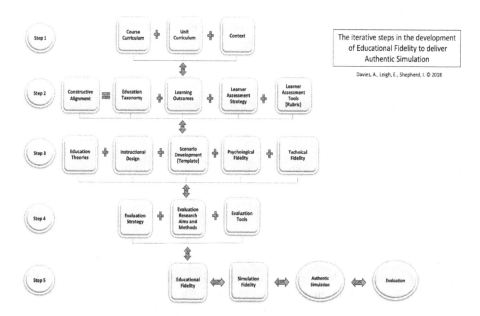

Fig. 1. The ADELIS© model

Leigh [23] notes that knowledge generated through application (e.g. design and use of simulation and simulation-related equipment) is especially susceptible to time constraints. Conversely knowledge acquired through analysis and research (theorising) is concerned with verifying truth and exploring implications requiring longer time frames to produce relevant results. Shepherd [7] has identified that while authors discuss various education theories and their relationship to simulation there is a dearth of reported applications using frameworks. In this paper the focus is on introducing a way of aligning relevant learning and educational theory with appropriate practice in the simulation field.

The authors apply the ADELIS© model, to guides users towards establishing a level of educational fidelity, ensuring the simulation intervention is valid, reliable and reproducible – from both a learning and assessment perspective. The iterative steps in the ADELIS© model, with their interconnecting cues and clues, contribute to the logical development of an authentic learning activity, when used with appropriate understanding of related knowledge. When the process is followed and activities are developed, there are opportunities to measure (a) the intervention itself, (b) immediate learning and behaviours in context, and (c) the impact of the exercise as considered from the educator's and the participant's perspective, as well as (d) broader organisational concerns.

5.1 Step 1

Step 1 invites educators to identify which elements in a course or curriculum unit lend themselves to use of simulation. A mapping exercise within and across units of a course is worthwhile, as it indicates the possible scope for a series of simulations to support scaffolding of knowledge acquisition and skill development. This step enables consideration of the context of each simulation, and possible connectivities and interplays among simulations and other learning processes. It uses the Cynefin Domains to help identify appropriate knowledge sets.

5.2 Step 2

Building on the outcomes of Step 1, Step 2 requires educators to apply a constructive alignment process to identify and develop Learning Outcomes using relevant action verbs from an education taxonomy such as Bloom's Taxonomy [24]. Once the Learning Outcomes are composed, appropriate assessment strategies tasks and tools are selected. Since choice of an effective assessment is the focus of this application of the ADELIS© model the following information explicitly links core outcomes of a simulation activity to the assessment element of the whole process.

5.3 Assessment

Assessment in this context relates to measurement of knowledges, skills and attitudes acquired or amended by learners as a result of participation in a simulation. Using an educational framework to guide the construction of a simulation not only allows all aspects of design, delivery and evaluation to occur, it guides how assessment criteria and processes can be developed. Understanding education theories underpinning simulation allows developers to identify and address factors concerned with education theories, a partial list of which is included in Table 2. As there is significant and constant interplay among all the theories listed in Table 2, it is vital that developers are aware of how these interrelationships might evolve as participants undergo contextualised assessment in a simulated environment. The critical fundamental objective is for authenticity of assessment to parallel the education intervention and that it matches the level of learning undertaken by participants. Hence appropriate constructive alignment must first identify appropriate learning outcomes and align them to relevant assessment tasks. The approach includes various triggers to ensure the process follows the logic of the education framework.

Table 2. Education theory - core/related concepts

Education theories	Core/related concepts
About teaching/learning processes	Pedagogy, Andragogy, Heutagogy
About kinds of knowledge	Tacit/Implicit/Explicit knowledge
About thinking skills	Critical thinking, Decision making, Clinical reasoning/Reflective practice
About capability development	Skill development, Acquiring expertise
About personal awareness	Self-efficacy, Interpersonal relationships

5.4   Step 3

Once this is established, Step 3 focuses on developing appropriate content to address learning outcomes and delivery processes. Here the developer has to consider which education theories underpin and address learning outcomes and assessment criteria [7]. Then scenario development and refinement occurs, using an instructional design approach. In this phase consideration is given to the levels of psychological and technical fidelity required to encourage participant to buy into the fiction contract [7].

5.5   Step 4

Step 4 focuses on the evaluation strategy and associated processes to determine the efficacy and relevance of the simulation activity. Here the designer needs to determine aims and methods of associated research and identify and provide validated and reliable evaluation tools.

5.6   Evaluation

Establishing an evaluation strategy for a simulation exercise and environment is pivotal to design, financial and human resourcing, sustainability, and ultimately learning efficiency and efficacy. However, the reality is that including a means of evaluating learning factors is often an afterthought, separated from discussions for the simulation exercise and environment itself. A significant level of work has been conducted across a range of professions pursuing best practice assessment of learning in and with simulation exercises [5, 9, 25, 26]. However, a less developed area is the evaluation of a simulation's adequacy for enabling learning and the learner's ability to transition from simulated experience to application in the relevant field of practice.

Our evaluation model was developed by Davies [9] and consists of four (4) phases. Table 3 summarises the four (4) phase evaluation process, and contextualises it in the ADELIS© mode. The four (4) phases loosely align to the Kirkpatrick's [27–29] four phases of - Reaction: evaluating participants responses to training; Learning: measuring what was learnt; Behaviour: consideration of post-training usage and performance; Results: evaluating if and to what extent learning has impacted the learner and organisation. The adapted approach embraces the emerging trend of applying a triangulated data collection strategy in the field of learning technology to generate rich, context-dependent information based on lived experiences and underpinned by robust quantitative data analysis. The model guides evaluation towards closing the gap between practitioners, educationalists and researchers, through enabling identification and analysis of the 'practical' aspects of the simulation design and the identification and analysis of associated learning theory in simulation-based learning.

5.7   Step 5

The final step in the ADELIS© model provides a protocol by which simulation developers can identify that educational fidelity has been achieved. Using a pre-delivery checklist, the educator/developer identifies and confirms that all appropriate elements have been identified, providing assurance that the simulation has achieved overall simulation fidelity and authenticity.

The ADELIS© model, and its iterative steps including the action research cycle approach, provides a logical, evidence-based educationally focused approach, not previously explored in the literature on design and use of simulation. Such an iterative process guides the user along an educational design path ensuring educational fidelity underpinned by educational theory and enhancing simulation design and improved capability outcomes of the activity.

Table 3. Evaluation Process and Example Concepts

Phase 1: Aims of the evaluation

Identify the aims of the evaluation – what do you want to know?
- Identify what are the learning outcomes?
- Identify the commencing level of knowledge and skills of the learner
- Identify expectations of Instructors for the learners and the simulation exercise and environment
- Identify the data collection tools
    - learner surveys pre and post training, field-based interviews and surveys
    - Instructor pre and post training
    - Stakeholder field-based interviews and or surveys
- Identify distribution of the findings and continuous improvement process

Phase 2: Adequacy of the simulation exercise and environment

Identify the expectations for the simulation exercise and environment to enable learners to apply their learning
- Identify the measurement criteria by which the adequacy of the simulation exercise and environment design can be reliably measured
- Identify survey questions for learners and instructors which will capture the data to respond to identifying the extent to which the exercise and environment allowed for application of learning
- Identify what is important – immersion, presence, engagement, realism, contextualisation of learning

Phase 3: Influence on transfer of learning to the field of practice

Identify the field-based practice to be demonstrated by learners
- Identify the field-based measurement protocols to be applied to determine if and to what extent transfer of learning has occurred
- Identify the survey and field-based interview questions for learners which enable reflection of the influence of the simulation exercise and environment on confidence to apply learning in the real world of their professional practice
- Identify the survey and field-based interview questions for stakeholders which enable measurement of the learners' field-based application of learning
- Identify the survey and interview questions for learners which enables reflection on the realism and adequacy of the simulation exercise and environment from the now real-world perspective

Phase 4: Analysis and reporting

Key areas for analysis and reporting include (but not limited to):
- Adequacy of the simulation-based exercise context and content to support learning objectives
- Adequacy of the simulation scenario to contextualise application of learning
- Influence of the simulation elements to support learning e.g. noise, light, tactile characteristics
- Adequacy of the simulation exercise to support learning transfer

6 Case Studies

The following case studies illustrate application of the ADELIS© model to existing programs with simulation-based learning activities. In the first case study the process of working through the four steps of the ADELIS© model in reference to an existing program of learning enables an informed basis from which to re-engineer the individual elements where required. The process also builds the knowledge and skill of staff for transfer to developing new simulation-based learning exercises within education and training programs. In the second case study an existing unit of study in an undergraduate International Business studies course is 'retrofitted' to the ADELIS© model, as a way of demonstrating that good practice is inevitably well-sourced with relevant educational theory.

6.1 Case Study 1

The context is a virtual reality decision-making simulation environment for 'shoot/don't shoot' law enforcement education; use of a decision-making simulation environment. Learners are placed in situations requiring application of knowledge and skills associated with use of firearms as one component of a comprehensive program.

6.1.1 Step 1: Curriculum and Context
The program includes theory and practice. Here the theory, validated through research and underpinned by associated literature, is centred on participants developing and applying knowledge of the influencing elements in the decision-making process including: study of human rights, ethics, law, communication and conflict management theory, police/law enforcement procedures. The practical training includes drills associated with handling and engaging a firearm, situational awareness, and physical de-escalation skills.

6.1.2 Step 2: Constructive Alignment
In this case the learning outcomes are associated with demonstration of application of the capability to draw together the core course theory and skills. The learning assessment strategies are identified as (1) those which indicate the learner has demonstrated application of an appropriate decision-making model (inclusive of consideration of the influencing elements) (2) those which indicate the learner has applied the correct firearm and safety skills (Fig. 2). Program and course learning outcomes

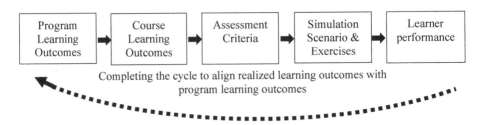

Fig. 2. Constructive alignment cycle

were pre-set, so the work for alignment was to ensure the scenario and assessment measurements met program and course learning outcomes.

6.1.3 Step 3: Education Theories

Learner participation in a simulation, the environment of which enables them to actively assimilate new information, explore the learning experience, facilitated by a teacher/instructor aligns with the education theory of cognitive constructivism [30]. The instructional design for the simulation aligns enabling opportunities for the learner to experience an environment in which they are able to apply learnt knowledge and skills to discover and then reflect on their actual application. Inclusion of instructor/ teacher facilitation of the experience offers an avenue to guide the learning and reflection. In this case, the design of the scenario with associated psychological and technical fidelity provides relevant realistically based police response situations. In a 2013 evaluation study of the simulation, 370 learners from a cohort of 372, agreed the scenarios were realistic. Further, 371 of the learners agreed they were able to apply their knowledge and skills in the simulation [12].

6.1.4 Step 4: Evaluation

A comprehensive evaluation strategy was implemented utilizing the process outlined in Table 3 with the analysis of the data contributing to continuous improvement of the overall program. Two of the most significant findings were centred on the connectivity between the virtual and real environment and transitioning to workplace contexts the learning gained by engaging in simulation-based learning activity.

Learners were surveyed pre and post simulation participation, followed by a field-based survey and interview when officers graduated to operational police officers. An example of the data collected is in Table 4. This data contributes to understanding the adequacy of the scenario design in creating an authentic learning environment. Similarly, the data presented in Table 5 offers insight into the level of realism experienced by the learners in the simulated scenario environment. As suggested in Phase 3 of the evaluation process, collecting data from the learners' real-world operational practice post simulation participation offers valuable insight into the level of influence of the simulation-based learning activity (and individual components). To collect this data, learners, their field-based work supervisors, and course instructors were surveyed and interviewed to establish a balanced perspective for evaluating the simulation-based learning activity. An example of the data collected is offered in Tables 4 and 5.

Table 4. Learner perspective on the scenario alignment to real world situations

Post simulation experience survey	Very strongly agree	Strongly agree	Agree
I consider the scenario depicted in the simulation was reflective of real situations	38%	43%	19%

Table 5. Level of realism experienced by participants

The simulation scenarios made me feel as if I were actually at the scene in real time	Very strongly agree	Strongly agree	Agree	Undecided	Disagree	Strongly disagree	Very strongly disagree
	53 (14.2%)	87 (23.4%)	126 (33.9%)	46 (12.4%)	38 (10.2%)	9 (2.4%)	13 (3.5%)

In this study the evaluation process was comprehensive, followed the 4-phase evaluation process and produced findings which are an important contribution to the quality assurance cycle of this program and advocating for simulation-based learning.

6.2   Case Study 2

6.2.1   Step 1: Curriculum and Context

The particular unit of study is a three-week intensive program occurring early in a two and a half-year undergraduate program. The degree is taught in English, and was established 30 years ago when the host country (a non-English speaking country) was just beginning to consider the value and validity of undergraduate teaching in English. The subject is called 'Introduction to Management' and intends - as the title suggests - to introduce concepts of management to newly arriving undergraduates.

The current version of the course was first presented in 2016 at a time when staff changes meant there was an opportunity to trial new learning design processes. The subject is being presented as a form of 'classroom as organisation' - a process involving students in direct management of classroom processes including much that is traditionally considered to be the role of the educator.

6.2.2   Step 2: Constructive Alignment

Alignment in this case study initially required understanding of the overall course of study before settling into design of the unit of study. The present situation is that the subject matches the overall course goals of engagement, work readiness and theoretically sound content. It varies somewhat from the majority of the other units in the way that students are expected to engage directly with the practice of management as they explore the theory. For some this seems more difficult due to a perceived need to rely on the educator to tell them what to do and what it is important to 'know'.

The subject is built in alignment with educational theories promoting thinking skills, capability development and self-awareness. That is, the teaching/learning process requires that students pay as much attention to what they are doing - each moment - as they pay attention to what they are reading. It is designed to help learners attend to the fact that theory is drawn from observations of practice and cannot be usefully considered separately from behaviour.

6.2.3   Step 3: Education Theories - Enacting Step 3 of the ADELIS© Model

To achieve a contextual embedding of abstract theory into guidelines for personal action, the unit aligns with components of Stage 3 of the ADELIS© model in the following ways:

1. Instructional Design - materials and instructions align along two dimensions of (a) core management theory concepts, and (b) within a framework replicating an action learning cycle [31].
2. Scenario Development - the scenario making this a simulation requires students to think of themselves as members of an organisation (much like a business start-up) with appropriately designated roles and responsibilities.
3. Psychological Fidelity - as much as possible the educator becomes a Senior Manager - or Chairman of the Board with designated roles and responsibilities that do not include 'teaching' and are described as 'giving advice, support, coaching and guidance'. Thus, participants are required to think themselves into role as contributors to a 'living organisation' whose product is the quality and content of their own learning as indicated by completion of relevant assessment tasks and daily routines providing peer support and contributing directly to the knowledge quotient expected to be acquired through completion of the unit of study.
4. Technical Fidelity - this is limited by the fact that everything takes place in a classroom, and relies on typical equipment to be found in an educational rather than a business setting. These limitations are addressed through use of various 'props' such that the room is re-set away from conventional rows of tables and chairs, and is set up using cafe-style clusters of furniture and equipment.

6.2.4   Step 4: Evaluation

Current evaluation strategies are limited to conventional end of course reviews. Students indicate varying capacities to accept that theory and practice are a duality and that their learning must eventually embrace the need to demonstrate a capacity to act and well as think and remember. This is subject to ongoing analysis and research.

A recent document reviewing progress to date indicates that:

> In future consider the issue as a process of helping students learn to respect their own - and their peers - capabilities. Looking inward and around rather than up and out! Questions arising include; how do educators learn to respect their learners? and how can they help learners better respect their own knowledge (and that of their peers) while also adding to it? (Source: Unpublished correspondence 2017).

7   Conclusion

What does this mean for the many practitioners who work in unpredictable domestic and global educational landscapes? The ADELIS© model provides users with an opportunity to positively impact on closing the gap between educational theories and practical processes involved in the design, delivery and evaluation of simulation-based learning activities. This is particularly important in any context where the expectation is that a simulation will add to and enhance the knowledge base, skill set, attitude, resilience and thus employability of participants. It is also important, from an industry perspective, that the educational development of both the simulation practitioner and their participants is validly addressing their respective needs and demands.

We provide an educational framework to bring together a range of relevant evidence-based education theories and models identified as central to the use of simulation as a learning, teaching and assessment method. Following establishment of the need and context, we propose the use of the ADELIS© model's step by step approach to guide the educator towards designing their simulation to provide an improved level of educational fidelity, training delivery, assessment validity and longer term evaluation of outcome of simulation-based learning exercises.

This paper outlines steps to help bridge the gap between proponents of sound educational theories and those who implement training technology. Experiences designed using the ADELIS© model can incorporate the latest technology, include educational methodologies to ensure maximum skill transfer, and allow for increased monitoring of performance. Whether the training scenario is for new knowledge and clinical practice, skillset maintenance, or focused on clinical human factor development and assessment, following the recommended steps during scenario development will help ensure that training provides the maximum number of benefits to healthcare professionals. This will have a flow-on effect in all aspects of workplace outcomes.

This strategy and process is designed to mitigate the gap between educational theory and simulation activity so that participants have simulation experiences where the knowledge and skills are clearly interconnected and interdependent. As educators we want to ensure that learning objectives in all settings are appropriately addressed and that participants have opportunities to effectively and successfully achieve relevant learning outcomes and human attributes. In this way we are contributing to the overall development and quality improvement of simulation-based learning across all contexts. Our case studies demonstrate how the model can be contextualised to any discipline where simulation is a teaching and learning method.

References

1. Lewin, K.: A Dynamic Theory of Personality. McGraw Hill, New York (1935)
2. Manning, S., Reinecke, J.: We're failing to solve the world's 'wicked problems.' Here's a better approach. The Conversation (2016). https://theconversation.com/were-failing-to-solve-the-worlds-wicked-problems-heres-a-better-approach-64949
3. Snowden, D.J., Boone, M.E.: A leader's framework for decision making. Harv. Bus. Rev. **85**, 69–76 (2007)
4. Shepherd, I., Burton, T.: A conceptual framework for simulation in healthcare education- the need. Nurs. Educ. Today **76**, 21–25 (2019)
5. Davies, A.: Beyond the Tick and Flick: an approach to identifying the realised value of simulation exercises in educating for the future. Int. J. Innov. Res. Educ. Sci. **2**(3), 116–119 (2015)

6. Leigh, E.: A Practitioner Researcher Perspective on Facilitating an Open, Infinite, Chaordic Simulation. (EdD), University of Technology Sydney, Sydney (2003). https://opus.lib.uts.edu.au/handle/2100/308
7. Shepherd, I.: A conceptual framework for simulation in healthcare education, (EdD) Victoria University Research Repository (2017). http://vuir.vu.edu.au/35047/
8. Adamson, K.A., Kardong-Edgren, S.: A method and resources for assessing the reliability of simulation evaluation instruments. Nurs. Educ. Perspect. **33**(5), 334–339 (2012)
9. Davies, A.: A Model for Evaluating the Impact of Simulation based Learning Environments. Australasian Simulation Congress, Melbourne, Simulation Australasia (2017)
10. Bloomberg: The Bloomberg recruiter report: Job skills companies want but can't get (2015). https://www.bloomberg.com/graphics/2015-job-skills-report/
11. Jackson, D.A., Chapman, E.: Non-technical skill gaps in Australian business graduates. Educ. Train. **54**(2/3), 95–113 (2012). https://doi.org/10.1108/00400911211210224
12. Davies, A.: What is the impact of simulation-based learning exercises on the development of decision-making skills and professional identity in operational policing? Doctoral thesis, Charles Sturt University, Wagga Wagga, Australia (2013)
13. Alinier, G., Platt, A.: International overview of high-level simulation education initiatives in relation to critical care. BACN Nurs. Crit. Care **19**, 1–8 (2013)
14. Davies (Dame), S.C.: A framework for technology enhanced learning, pp. 1–46. Crown, Department of Health Publications, London (2011). https://www.gov.uk/government/publications/a-framework-for-technology-enhanced-learning
15. Huang, Y.M., et al.: 2007 Simulation education summit. Simul. Healthc. **3**, 186–191 (2008)
16. Jeffries, P.R., Rogers, K.J.: Theoretical framework for simulation design. In: Jeffries, P.R. (ed.) Simulation in Nursing Education: From Conceptualization to Evaluation, p. 23. National League for Nursing, New York (2007)
17. Sadideem, H., Kneebone, R.: Practical skills teaching in contemporary surgical education: how can educational theory be applied to promote effective learning? Am. J. Surg. **204**(3), 396–401 (2012)
18. Harris, K.R., Eccles, D.W., Ward, P., Whyte, J.: A theoretical framework for simulation in nursing: answering Schiavenato's call. J. Nurs. Educ. **52**(1), 1–16 (2013)
19. Issenberg, B.S., Ringsted, C., Østergaard, D., Dieckmann, P.: Setting a research agenda for simulation- based healthcare education: a synthesis of the outcome from an Utstein style meeting. Simul. Healthc. **6**, 155–167 (2011)
20. Kaakinen, J., Arwood, E.: Systematic review of nursing simulation literature for use of learning theory. Education faculty publications and presentations. Paper 6 (2009)
21. Murdock, N.L.: Systematic literature review: a best practices review of simulated education approaches to enhance collaborative healthcare, MSN thesis, University of British Columbia, Okanagan, Canada (2012)
22. Pollard, M., Nickerson, M.: The use of multi-dimensional simulation to promote communication and collaboration in patient care. Power Point presentation, Exeter Hospital, Inc., Exeter, New Hampshire, USA (2011). http://connection.ebscohost.com/c/abstracts/65930430/abstracts-poster-presentations-use-multi-dimensional-simulation-topromote-communication-collaboration-patient-care
23. Leigh, E.: Bending time - using simulation to warp perceptions of time for learning purposes. In: Kaneda, T., Kanegae, H., Toyoda, Y., Rizzi, P. (eds.) Simulation and Gaming in the Network Society, vol. 9, pp. 13–24. Springer, Singapore (2015). https://doi.org/10.1007/978-981-10-0575-6_2
24. Iowa State University: Revised Blooms Taxonomy (2018). http://www.celt.iastate.edu/teaching/effective-teaching-practices/revised-blooms-taxonomy

25. Golling, M., Koch, R., Hillmann, P., Eiseler, V., Stiemert, L., Rekker, A.: On the evaluation of military simulations: towards a taxonomy of assessment criteria. Military Communications and Information Systems Conference (MilCIS), Canberra, Australia (2015). https://doi.org/10.1109/milcis.2015.7348943
26. Shepherd, I.A., Kelly, C.M., Skene, F.M., White, K.T.: Enhancing graduate nurses' health assessment knowledge and skills using low-fidelity adult human simulation. J. Soc. Simul. Health 2(1), 16–24 (2007)
27. Kirkpatrick, D.L.: Techniques for evaluating training programs. J. Am. Soc. Train. Dir. 11, 1–13 (1959)
28. Kirkpatrick, D.L.: Techniques for evaluating training programs. In: Kirkpatrick, D.L. (ed.) Evaluating Training Programs in Alexandria. ASTD, VA (1975)
29. Kirkpatrick, D.L.: Evaluating Training Programs. Berrett-Koehler Publishers Inc, San Francisco (1994)
30. Wadsworth, B.J.: Piaget's Theory of Cognitive and Affective Development: Foundations of Constructivism. Longman Publishing, White Plains (2004)
31. Dick, B.: Making process accessible: robust processes for learning, change and action research Practitioner theories. Paper 3. Action Research and Action Learning for community & organisational change (2002). http://www.aral.com.au/DLitt/index.html

Towards Optimizing Place Experience Using Design Science Research and Augmented Reality Gamification

Nikolche Vasilevski$^{(\boxtimes)}$ ⓘ and James Birt ⓘ

Bond University, 14 University Drive, Robina, Gold Coast, QLD 4226, Australia
nvasilev@bond.edu.au

Abstract. Studies suggest that augmented reality and game mechanics can lead to increase sense of place. This is important as sense of place provides many benefits ranging from personal place significance, to increase interest and stewardship at the place. These benefits combined can lead to enhancement of an offered service. Therefore, the question asked in this research is how to effectively design an experience using these emerging technologies and optimize for successful outcomes? In this study we outline the design and development process of a pervasive mobile application solution using design science research methodology guidelines to answer this question. Specifically, the application solution replicates a human guide and narration experience in the exhibition of indigenous artworks in a university place by integrating augmented reality, micro location, audio and enhancement through gamification service to increase engagement and experience value. We present observation result data from the first iteration of the design science research methodology by analyzing qualitative usability testing of the application by expert stakeholders. The results indicate that the performance usability of the app is satisfactory, and it provides solid base for the next iteration of the development process.

Keywords: Sense of place · Augmented reality · Gamification ·
Design science research

1 Introduction

The concept of Place in the literature is challenged, however generally defined as a location that has a meaning [1]. Sense of Place (SoP) is a scientific construct that undergoes much debate in the academy and has been defined from different perspectives and in various disciplines [7].

For the purpose of our research we look at SoP from the attitude theory perspective, where Jorgensen and Stedman [12] define SoP as "multidimensional construct comprising: beliefs about the relationship between self and place; feelings toward the place; and the behavioral exclusivity of the place in relation to alternatives". These three dimensions are evident in the literature as *place identity*, *place attachment* and *place dependence*.

© Springer Nature Singapore Pte Ltd. 2019
A. Naweed et al. (Eds.): ASC 2019, CCIS 1067, pp. 77–92, 2019.
https://doi.org/10.1007/978-981-32-9582-7_6

SoP therefore, attaches meaning to a place and provides many benefits to the place itself, such as caring for the place, prolonging the stay or investing in the place [5]. Increasing SoP will lead to increase in the benefits for the place.

The literature shows that performing activities at a place increases SoP, and even more if these activities are joyful and engaging with the place. Performing augmented reality (AR) activities or having gameful experiences at place can also increase SoP [5, 17]. These two methods, AR and gamification are the primary focus of this research.

AR as the name suggests is referred to as a structure of overlaying virtual objects over real-world objects, attached to and bound by the three dimensions of the real world and which is in the same time interactive [2]. The advances in the technology led to miniaturization and increase computational power to run the AR applications on handheld smartphone devices and wearables such as AR glasses. AR requires a link to the real world to work, and that link is provided by the three essential technologies for AR, which are tracking, display and input [3].

AR has been shown as a way for pointing to real world objects and as a precise location system, Google Maps app is using for precise navigation as their Visual Positioning System (VPS) at places with low GPS signal reception, such as city centers [13]. This system is independent and free from some major GPS location shortcomings, such as indoor positioning and granularity [14].

The system also employs iBeacon [14] technology for micro-location and proximity computation. This technology uses small devices called beacons, which act as lighthouses transmitting signal that can be detected by Bluetooth Low Energy capable devices and computed into distance from the beacon. This usable distance varies from few centimeters to ~ 50 m depending on the surroundings and the obstacles. The distance to a beacon is divided into three distinct proximity regions: immediate, near and far. This type of micro location technology has been successfully applied in various gamification scenarios within different implementations [21].

The other concept that may lead to increase in SoP is gamification. Gamification is referred to as using game like features in non-gaming context [6]. Furthermore, Huotari and Hamari [10] ground the definition in service marketing, defining it as, "a process of enhancing a service with affordances for gameful experiences in order to support users' overall value creation". This perspective has many implications of how gamification can be used towards specific goals related to service enhancement.

Service marketing is postulated on Service-Dominant Logic (S-DL) [19], where the value of the product is not created by the manufacturer, but only by the consumers that consumes the products. In this paradigm, the human skills are more valuable than natural resources [20]. "Any intentional act – no matter how small – that assists an entity can be considered a service" [10] and any organized array of services can be considered a service system.

A service system can be considered any partnership, organization, a part of an organization, club and even the basic human organizational unit as the family. To help businesses manage the services, a service package model was introduced to S-DL, which categorizes the services into three groups: core, enabling and enhancing service [8]. For instance, in public transport, the core service is transportation, the enabling service is buying a ticket, and enhancing service is Wi-Fi onboard the bus. As per the definition gamification is considered an enhancing service of an already present core service. It should also be noted that a game can be considered a gamified implementation if it is used to enhance a core service, for instance playing *PokemonGo* app (www.pokemongo.com) in a retail shop.

Gamification increases engagement and makes activities joyful and interesting. In most of the cases, successful gamification implementations implement treasure/scavenger hunt scenarios, where the main game mechanics used are badges, points and leaderboards [21]. Gamification of micro-location (GM-L) is a subset of gamification of location-based services, which is already a researched SoP predictor [18, 23].

The goals of our greater study are to answer two main research questions; (i) can deploying GM-L increase SoP, and (ii) how designers and developers can optimize for successful outcomes. In this paper we focus on answering the latter of the research questions that is the designing for optimized and successful outcomes. To achieve this, we first present the design science research methodology used in the study, followed by the qualitative usability results and the discussions with expert stakeholders. Finally, at the end we present the conclusions and the future work.

2   Methodology

This section presents the methodology used in this phase of the research, towards answering the research question: "How developers optimize for successful outcomes?". We designed, tested and evaluated our solution in several iterations, by following the Design Science Research Methodology (DSRM) [15]. This approach led to development of a Gamified AR Micro-location (GARM-L) artefact, in the form of a mobile app, that initially deployed iBeacon beacons, smartphone AR, and synthesized voice narration. The human voice narration and game mechanics were added later on in the development process.

2.1   Solution Design and Implementation

The solution consists of GARM-L mobile app, in which the first component is a narrated AR tour guide solution for an indigenous artwork tour in an Australian university setting. The second component is a gamified solution where the players (users of the GARM-L) have to discover the hidden features on the paintings through AR.

The first iteration of the solution focused on the AR component only, due to complexity of the development of an artifact that will be a high-quality app, which itself would not have any significant effect on SoP. The AR component was developed in the Unity game engine. The application was engineered as a multiplatform app, that can be installed and run on both, iOS and Android OS platforms, and it has identical functionality and aesthetics on both.

The AR component relied on the Vuforia AR engine embedded within Unity, specifically, Vuforia single image targets. To use the engine, a unique API key was used and entered in Unity Editor Inspector. The Vuforia AR image targets were the indigenous paintings from the real-world tour. The targets were created by uploading hi-resolution photos of the paintings on Vuforia developer's website where the primary features are identified for augmentation and imported as an image target database in Unity.

The initial design of the application was constructed by following the design of several major AR enabled museum apps that incorporate tour guidance. We scanned the two major app stores, Apple AppStore and Google PlayStore for the baseline application.

We initially searched by the term (museum AND tour AND guide AND AR). This search only returned 16 apps, and most of which were not in the specific context. Therefore, we adjusted the search for the less specific search term (museum AND tour), which returned 214 apps on AppStore and 242 on the Google PlayStore. Most of the apps from the search were available on both platforms. We had to scan the app info and description in the store listings for the apps and determine initial relevant apps. We excluded the payed apps, due to not offering any extra design patterns over the free ones, which was evident from the store screenshots. We selected 23 apps that matched the criteria of having a tour guidance, location awareness, and narration and installed these apps on an Apple iPhoneX smartphone. All these apps were available on both the iPhone and android operating systems. Also, in addition, we downloaded the Mona O app, only available on AppStore, due to the unique micro-location technology implementation.

After performing the testing, we narrowed down the selection to six apps, that were applying design patterns applicable for our specific use case. These apps were: (i) *The O* (mona.net.au/museum/the-o), (ii) *Australian museum* (australianmuseum.net.au/visit/mobile-apps/), (iii) *Palace* (en.chateauversailles.fr/discover/resources/palace-versailles-application), (iv) *Louvre Guide* (www.museumtourguides.com/home/), and (v) *Dali Museum* (www.acoustiguide.com/tours-apps/tour=dali-museum-virtual-tour/) (Fig. 1).

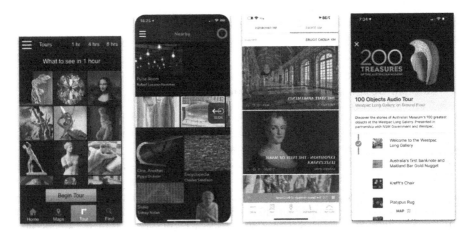

Fig. 1. Screenshots of the selected apps. From left to right: *Louvre Guide, The O, Dali Museum, Australian Museum.*

After the content and design examination of the selected apps, the initial interviews with experts and several prototypes, we came up with the initial design of the app. It should be noted that an indigenous culture expert approved the design of the app as culturally sensitive and sensible. The initial version of the app (V1) consisted of the following screens: Main, Tour, Gallery, Artwork Info, Map, AR, Badges, and About. The wireframes are presented in (Fig. 2).

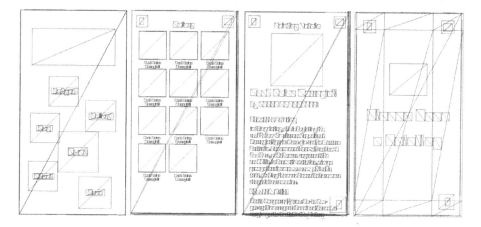

Fig. 2. App v1 Wireframes from left to right: Main, Gallery, Artwork Info, AR

The first version of the app color scheme was black background, with white accents and white typography. The buttons on the main screen were representing motifs from indigenous paintings and also the title font was the Aboriginal Alphabet font by the artist Araki Koman (Fig. 3). The fonts used throughout the app were one of the default fonts from Unity Engine called Nexa and Nexa – Bold.

Fig. 3. App v1 Main screen

The logic flow of the first app iteration was as follows; After starting the app, users would be first taken to the main screen, where they will be presented with the circular buttons with indigenous motifs that on click would take them to the respective screens. Every screen has a back to the previous screen option. The flow of the app use is presented on the following flowchart (Fig. 4).

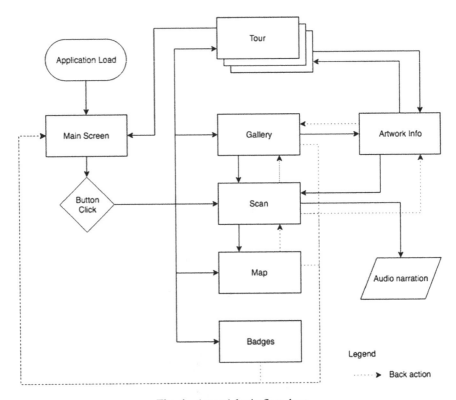

Fig. 4. App v1 logic flowchart

The Tour screen presented the user with guided tour, which in essence was a series of the Artwork Information screens, ordered to represent the real-world tour sequence (Fig. 5). On the first, welcome to the tour, screen the user started the tour by tapping on the Start Tour button. Next, the screen for the first painting of the tour appeared, which offered the choice of augmenting the painting through AR, listening to the audio narration, reading about the painting through the artwork info, advancing to the next painting. The choice to use both audio and text was to reduce cognitive load and offer a dual coding scheme to enhance user comprehension.

There was a choice of going back to the previous painting from the second painting onwards. The users would manually advance to the next painting in their own time allowing for a self-directed experience. The tour ends after the user would tap on the end tour button presented on the final painting tour screen.

Fig. 5. App v1 Tour and Artwork info screens

The Gallery screen is presenting all the paintings in the walk in three column vertical thumbnails grid, a back button, title and AR scan button (Fig. 6). This layout was inspired by the *Louvre Guide* and *The O* apps, and it is a pragmatic take on the presentation of the paintings in the most accessible way to the user. The thumbnails are filled fully by the painting which is resized to fit the square shape.

We experimented with preserving the ratio of the thumbnails, however it is inconsistent and not aesthetically pleasing. A tap on the painting would take the user to the info screen. Artwork info screen is scrollable single column, full width list, that contains the larger image of the painting, and information about the painting (Fig. 6).

Initially, there was an option of presenting a fullscreen image of the painting by tapping on the image, however that option was abandoned due to causing copyright infringement. The order of the list is, top-down, the painting image, title of the painting, author name, About the painting section and About the author section. There were also three buttons, a back, AR scan and narration button. Tap on the narration button would narrate the About the painting section with Apple's Karen, Australian female synthesized voice. The background color of this screen is dark gray, which as per Android material design guidelines, gives the feel of depth, as the lighter color than black represents the layer that is closer to the user.

The AR screen was accessible directly from the Main, Gallery and Artwork info screens. Its main purpose was to present to the user the meaning of the features on the paintings from the tour. This was possible by scanning the paintings by the main camera of the smartphone.

Fig. 6. App v1 Gallery screen and Artwork info screen with audio narration playing

The screen had two display options: target-scanning and target-found modes (Fig. 7). Both modes had three buttons, two leading back and to the Gallery screen, and one for audio narration. The narration button was only visible in target-found mode.

Fig. 7. App v1 AR screen, target-scanning and target-found modes

When one of the tour paintings entered in the field of view of the main camera, the Vuforia engine was able to recognize it as a target and trigger the target-found mode. In target-found mode the user was able to see the title of the painting and the names of the painting's features.

The Map, Badges and About screens were not developed for this version due the fact we did not consider these features crucial for this iteration of the development process which was to test the augmentation. Placeholder items are presented on Fig. 8.

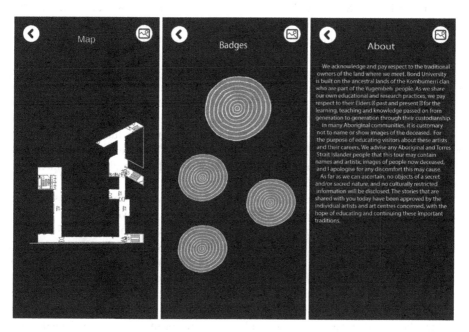

Fig. 8. App v1 Map, Badges and About placeholder screens

2.2 Meetings with the Experts

We organized the initial meetings with the selected experts and the stakeholders from the authors institution, where we presented our initial design ideas, the goal and the objectives of the solution and recorded their feedback which was in line with the DSR methodology.

This iteration sample size was five (n = 5) experts, part of the core experts group were, an Indigenous culture expert (Indigenous artist), User-experience expert (Advertisement firm director), Service-marketing expert (Partnerships Manager at the Office of Alumni and Development), Sense of Place expert (PHD researcher and experienced local government representative in the School of Architecture), Exhibit organization expert (Curator of the indigenous walk at the authors institution). This sample of experts represents the larger institutional stakeholder group.

There was no official quantitative usability testing conducted with the stakeholders with only qualitative data recorded in the form of their requirements, expectations, thoughts and important points regarding the app, during open-ended interviews.

2.3 Simulation and Usability Testing

The initial evaluation of the application prior to testing with the experts was performed in a simulated environment by the research and development team. Testing was conducted using both iOS and Android devices, including iPhone X, XS Max, and SE, Samsung Galaxy S6, S7 and S8. Testing was performed to validate the usability of the initial builds of the app and establish the baselines for future usability testing in line with the DSR methodology.

The final build was stable and performed as expected on both platforms optimizing for the experience. Six paintings, of the total 35 tour paintings were randomly chosen and imported into the Unity Project. These paintings were uploaded to the Vuforia developer's website, where it generated the targets and the library, which was also imported into the project. We also used GPS and iBeacon to evaluate the accuracy of the technologies within the building. The GPS proved to be extremely ineffective and inconsistent to be of use, while the iBeacon beacons offered usable performance to associate the user to the location.

After the development of the alpha build of the app v1 as the first phase of the software development cycle where usability testing begins [11], we conducted usability testing with the experts and recorded their feedback. The testing was conducted by using observation and interviews with open-ended questions [16]. We handed the experts the app installed on Apple iPhone X smartphone and presented a portfolio folder containing A4 prints of the six paintings. Following the introduction of the app and presenting the features and how to use them, we observed how the tester used the app. The testers were using the app autonomously and we only intervened when asked to. Once they finished testing all the available features of the app, we conducted semi-structured interviews and recorded the conversations.

Near the end of the interviews we presented the experts with the five sample applications to the experts and recorded their comments in regard to the developed Corrigan Walk tour app and the contrast with the existing applications from the app store.

To assess usability we adapted the usability questionnaire from Hoehle, Aljafari and Venkatesh [9] as a set of ten focal points for the usability testing and interview structure. The concepts that we focused on during the testing are the following:

(i)   Aesthetic graphics - regarding mobile application's artwork, rich, beautiful, engaging graphics and good design;
(ii) Color – regarding mobile application appropriate use or misuse of colors and contrast;
(iii) Control obviousness – regarding the mobile app consistent use of controls and obviousness of apps goals;
(iv) Entry point – regarding the ways the mobile app accessibility (icon, menu);

   (v) Fingertip-size controls – regarding the mobile app use of controls and buttons in terms of size;

  (vi) Font – regarding the mobile app use of a good font and font size;

 (vii) Gestalt – regarding the mobile app handling proximity and grouping;

(viii) Hierarchy – regarding the mobile app use of a clear hierarchy and structure;

  (ix) Subtle animation – regarding the mobile app use of animations effectively and appropriately;

   (x) Transition – regarding the mobile app transitions and flow of the interface elements.

We also adapted several questions from Venkatesh and Davis [22] TAM2 Technology Acceptance Model as guidelines concerning the Usefulness in terms of how helpful, useful and effective the app is for the purposes of the tour.

AR component was further analyzed by following the five main types of AR evaluation techniques [3]: Objective measurements, Subjective measurements, Qualitative analysis, Usability evaluation techniques and Informal evaluations.

The interview data was analyzed by using thematic analysis [4]. Interview transcripts were coded regarding the concepts above, and additional themes were discovered and analyzed; Audio and Gamification.

3   Results and Discussions

In this section we present the results of the observation data and the thematic analysis of the semi-structured interviews conducted during the usability testing of the first build of the *Corrigan Walk Tour* app v1. The results following the previously described usability concepts of: Aesthetic graphics, Color, Control, Entry, Fingertip-size, Font, Gestalt, Hierarchy, Subtle animation, Transition, Usefulness guidelines and coded themes Audio, AR and Gamification.

The observation and the interview data showed that overall usability of the app was excellent. The user perceived quality of the app was on a high level. "It looks really professional" commented one of the testers. The app was responsive, did not freeze or crash during the testing and had no observable negative effects on the users. "It's very, very quick, very responsive." commented one of the testers, a few moments after using the app for the first time.

3.1   Aesthetic Graphics

All of the testers agreed that the aesthetics and graphics used in the app were enjoyable and engaging, by stating comments like: "…that's gorgeous, … Love it… I love the graphic look of it.", and "I'm very happy with the interface."

3.2   Color

Colors in the app were also praised by the testers, with comments such as "The color is, I think, is excellent." and "… (colors are) representative of all the artwork. I think that's a really good choice." Initially, the testers favored the white on black theme.

However, after the comparison with the other apps, some of the testers changed their opinions, favoring the black on white theme. Furthermore, one of the testers expressed concerns about the green color as one "…probably you don't see that as much in, …, in our Western desert." This was addressed by the indigenous art expert by pointing out that "…there is a lot of paintings that have the green (color)…"

3.3   Hierarchy

The users found the hierarchy to be easy to follow, and the app layout to be meaningful. However, one pointed out that there is a need of an integrated onboarding process saying: "I would like to be told, you can go on the tour, you can have audio, you can do that with this. Like, how can you tell some of what the capabilities of the app are before they start the tour?"

3.4   Control Obviousness

All of the testers were able to navigate the app, go to different screens and back with no help or extra effort allowing for a self-directed experience. Four of the testers found the navigation easy and intuitive, stating "I like the simplicity of it, and it's clear…. it seems like it would be easy to use and that anyone could use it." However, one tester had concerns about the layout of the Menu screen and even the need of one. She pointed out that all Main screen icon links may be integrated and available from the Tour screen, which subsequently might lead to shortening of the onboarding time. She also pointed out that there has to be an "acknowledgement about Aboriginal people before anything".

3.5   Font

The results showed mixed opinions about the font size and family, varying from "I wouldn't change anything about that…, …font is big enough." to "…it should be another couple of points smaller…, …just double check those fonts as well…" For the content text, on the other hand, all agreed that is appropriate, and also needs some separation between the paragraphs.

3.6   Fingertip-Size Controls

"Good size choice!" commented the UX expert, confirming that the size of the buttons was appropriate, and testers had no difficulties tapping on them, which was in agreement with the observation data.

3.7   Subtle Animation and Transition

At this stage of the development, there were no animations and transitions implemented. While some of the testers did not comment on this, some of them missed it "…there's no transition, you could add (it), if you wanted to pretty it up."

3.8   Audio

Concerning the audio narration, all testers agreed that the computer synthesized voice is not appropriate and that should be a real person's voice, preferably "…an Aboriginal person saying it…"

3.9   Augmented Reality

The AR component performed as expected. All the tested paintings were augmentable, the target recognition was responsive, and it could be used in different angles: "…it picks up real fast." and "…the scanning that's really clever".

3.10   Gamification

Regarding the planned gamification upgrade of the app, the opinions varied to extremes, where some of the testers did not see any value in it, some thought that introduction of game mechanics would vastly improve the engagement and motivation of the players.

3.11   Usefulness

All tests showed that the app was highly accessible. The interaction points and the content were easy to access, and the app suits both, left and right handed users. Testers were satisfied with the app capability of being able to achieve its goals, from the tour perspective and also from the study perspective.

To summarize, the overall experience and usability of the app was satisfactory, and majority of the testers agreed on that. Before and after reviewing the competitor apps, the experts came up with several ideas for additions or adjustments within the app, such as the color theme and the Menu screen.

Based on the results, presented above we can confirm that the AR component, as the first part of the solution, was conceptually validated by using the five types of AR evaluation techniques [3]. The first version build performed within the expectations, and it would provide a solid base for the integration of the second, the Gamification component. Unity Game Engine proved to be a reliable development tool for development of this type of applications, and testing or release on the both major mobile platforms, iOS and Android OS. The app v1 looks and performs identically on both platforms. The Vuforia AR engine also showed stability and integrity when employed, with fast and reliable recognition of the targets.

As the literature suggested, usability concepts, which we followed as pre-conceptualized guidelines proved very effective in regard of usability testing, as predicted in the literature [9].

The initial plan to place a beacon behind all the paintings proved to be unreliable solution to the micro-location granularity, due to the inconsistency of the transmitted signals and proximity detection, which required the user to bring the device very close to the beacon, to avoid interference from the neighboring beacons. This however would not be possible due to the required distance and field of view by the AR camera to recognize the target, because even the smallest painting is 1.5 m high. The unreliability of the beacons is not in complete agreement with the literature which shows various successful gamification of micro-location applications [21]. Probably this is due the specific requirements of this study, which we presented above, such as the minimum required distance from the paintings and the angles of scanning.

However, instead of solely the beacons, AR could be used as a micro-location provider during the AR scanning and then beacons would provide the micro-location within the segment of the space when not scanning. This solution would provide high granularity and precision within the closed spaces. Then micro-location would be used for navigation purposes. Due the shift from the iBeacon to AR as the main micro-location provider, this had strong effect on the design of the whole study, and it required adaptation of the pre and post, control group design, affecting the control group that was designed to use beacons to test the seamlessness of the iBeacon gamification of micro-location technology.

The expansion building works that were conducted at this time, in the building of the Health and Medicine Faculty, where the artworks for the tour are located, also affected the development speed and the real-world testing of the app. The interviews with the experts will influence the development of the next iterative build, with their suggestions about gamification and their separate opinions on the efficacy and necessity of GARM-L.

The app structure did not undergo major changes during the initial testing, and the two-scene approach proved valid, by separating the main content section from the AR scanning capability into separate scenes in Unity. The consistency between, and the stability on both mobile deployment platforms is a significant advantage.

4   Conclusion

This paper concludes the first iteration of the DSRM process as the last step which is dissemination of the knowledge. We present the development process, from the inception to the development of an alpha release of a mobile application artefact, as solution to the problem of researching the increase of SoP as a whole. The significance of this study can be found in its contribution to IS field by answering the research question "How developers optimize for successful outcomes?" and by providing a verified development procedure by following the DSRM guidelines, as the research methodology developed for IS solution development. This first iteration of the solution and the positive outcomes of the usability testing of the app v1, allow for the start of the next phase of the development.

The next phase will include improvements as result of usability testing and introduction of the second, the Gamification component as part of a GARM-L solution. We propose that the Gamification component to initially employ progress and badges as main game mechanics.

The paintings in AR will have hidden features (small areas) that player will have to discover by following the clues given through the voice narration. By tapping on the feature in AR, the feature will become visible and the player will be awarded a badge. Scanning the painting only, will be awarded as a separate badge. Finding all the badges will lead to receiving of a master badge, one for completion, and one for the features. Aesthetics and positions of the badges is still under discussed. We will also introduce a new Badges screen which will show the badges and the progress.

By taking the app outside the context of the main study, the possibilities of implementation of the app are many. The app is built to be flexible and easily scalable. It can be used in similar applications at places such as heritage sites, museums, galleries, fairs and all kinds of exhibitions. All these scenarios are possibilities of for future work and taking this study on the next level.

References

1. Agnew, J., Thrift, N.: Place and politics. The geographical mediation of state and society. Trans. Inst. Br. Geogr. **13**(2), 251 (1988). https://doi.org/10.2307/622518
2. Azuma, R.T.: A survey of augmented reality. Presence Teleoperators Virtual Environ. **6**(4), 355–385 (1997)
3. Billinghurst, M., Clark, A., Lee, G.: A survey of augmented reality. Found. Trends® Human–Computer Interact. **8**(2-3), 73–272 (2015)
4. Braun, V., Clarke, V.: Using thematic analysis in psychology. Qual. Res. Psychol. **3**(2), 77–101 (2006). https://doi.org/10.1191/1478088706qp063oa
5. Chang, Y.-L., Hou, H.-T., Pan, C.-Y., Sung, Y.-T., Chang, K.-E.: Apply an augmented reality in a mobile guidance to increase sense of place for heritage places. Educ. Technol. Soc. **18**(2), 166–178 (2015)
6. Deterding, S., Dixon, D., Khaled, R., Nacke, L.: From game design elements to gamefulness: defining gamification. In: Proceedings of the 15th International Academic MindTrek Conference: Envisioning Future Media Environments. ACM, New York (2011). https://doi.org/10.1145/2181037.2181040
7. Galliano, S.J., Loeffler, G.M.: Place assessment: how people define ecosystems. Gen. Technical rep. PNW-GTR-462, 31 (1999). https://doi.org/10.2737/PNW-GTR-462
8. Gronroos, C.: Service Management and Marketing: Customer Management in Service Competition, 3rd edn. Wiley, Hoboken (2007)
9. Hoehle, H., Aljafari, R., Venkatesh, V.: Leveraging Microsoft's mobile usability guidelines: conceptualizing and developing scales for mobile application usability. Int. J. Hum.-Comput. Stud. **89**, 35–53 (2016). https://doi.org/10.1016/j.ijhcs.2016.02.001
10. Huotari, K., Hamari, J.: A definition for gamification: anchoring gamification in the service marketing literature. Electron. Mark. **27**(1), 21–31 (2017). https://doi.org/10.1007/s12525-015-0212-z
11. Standard Glossary of Terms Used in Software Testing Version 3.2. https://www.istqb.org/downloads/send/20-istqb-glossary/186-glossary-all-terms.html. Accessed 5 May 2019

12. Jorgensen, B.S., Stedman, R.C.: Sense of place as an attitude: lakeshore owners attitudes toward their properties. J. Environ. Psychol. **21**(3), 233–248 (2001). https://doi.org/10.1006/jevp.2001.0226

13. Kaware, S.R.: Google maps with visual positioning system. IJSRCSEIT **3**(5), 310–315 (2018)

14. Newman, N.: Apple iBeacon technology briefing. J. Direct Data Digit. Mark. Pract. **15**(3), 222–225 (2014). https://doi.org/10.1057/dddmp.2014.7

15. Peffers, K., Tuunanen, T., Rothenberger, M.A., Chatterjee, S.: A design science research methodology for information systems research. J. Manag. Inf. Syst. **24**(3), 45–77 (2007). https://doi.org/10.2753/MIS0742-1222240302

16. User Interviews: How, When, and Why to Conduct Them. https://www.nngroup.com/articles/user-interviews/. Accessed 16 June 2019

17. Potts, R., Yee, L.: Pokémon Go-ing or staying: exploring the effect of age and gender on augmented reality game player experiences in public spaces. J. Urban Des., 1–18 (2019). https://doi.org/10.1080/13574809.2018.1557513

18. Sigala, M.: The application and impact of gamification funware on trip planning and experiences: the case of TripAdvisor's funware. Electron. Mark. **25**(3), 189–209 (2015). https://doi.org/10.1007/s12525-014-0179-1

19. Vargo, S.L., Lusch, R.F.: Evolving to a new dominant logic for marketing. J. Mark. **68**(1), 1–17 (2004). https://doi.org/10.1509/jmkg.68.1.1.24036

20. Vargo, S.L., Lusch, R.F., Archpru Akaka, M., He, Y.: Service-dominant logic. Review of Marketing Research, pp. 125–167. Emerald Group Publishing Limited (2010). https://doi.org/10.1108/S1548-6435(2009)0000006010

21. Vasilevski, N., Brand, J., Birt, J.: Analysing micro-location beacon gamification: scenarios, types and characteristics. In: Proceedings of the 30th Australian Conference on Computer-Human Interaction, pp. 484–489. ACM, New York (2018). https://doi.org/10.1145/3292147.3292210

22. Venkatesh, V., Davis, F.D.: A theoretical extension of the technology acceptance model: four longitudinal field studies. Manag. Sci. **46**(2), 186–204 (2000)

23. Xu, F., Tian, F., Buhalis, D., Weber, J.: Tourists as mobile gamers: gamification for tourism marketing. J. Travel. Tour. Mark. **33**(8), 1124–1142 (2016). https://doi.org/10.1080/10548408.2015.1093999

Search and Rescue

Simulation of an Unmanned Aerial Vehicle Search and Rescue Swarm for Observation of Emergent Behaviour

James B. Gibson⑩, John Page, and Faqihza Mukhlish$^{(\boxtimes)}$⑩

University of New South Wales, Kensington, NSW 2033, Australia
f.mukhlish@student.unsw.edu.au

Abstract. Swarms made up of many individual agents, can produce complex emergent behaviours that significantly exceed the capabilities of any individual agent. Emergent behaviours are commonly seen in nature, with birds, insects and other animals, and result from each agent following a simple rule set. The emergent behaviour can occur with or without awareness that a complex task is being completed.

The application of swarming principles to technology systems has been shown to be effective at increasing the efficiency of completing complex tasks. Past research has applied the principle of swarms to autonomous and semi-autonomous systems. While often successful, predicting the emergent behaviour of the swarm based on the rule sets given to the individual agents is difficult and often impossible. Instead swarms with a given rule set are simulated to determine if the emergent behaviour exhibited is the desired behaviour. However, there is potential that the level of sophistication of a simulation may effectively alter the agents rule set and hence the simulated emergent behaviour. This research develops a realistic simulation to compare with a less realistic simulation reported in similar work.

In this article, a search and rescue mission is simulated using up to eight unmanned aerial vehicle as the swarm. The simulation is set up using the Flight Gear Cluster Simulator at UNSW. The results of this research demonstrate that the emergent behaviour on the more realistic simulator is quite similar for a low number of agents but begin to differ for a larger number. It also shows that the unmanned aerial vehicles would tend to flock together in a similar manner to flocking birds, when over the centre of the search area, something not mentioned in the previous work.

Keywords: Swarms · Multi-agent · Emergent behaviour ·
Search and rescue simulation · Flocking

Supported by the University of New South Wales.

© Springer Nature Singapore Pte Ltd. 2019
A. Naweed et al. (Eds.): ASC 2019, CCIS 1067, pp. 95–105, 2019.
https://doi.org/10.1007/978-981-32-9582-7_7

1 Introduction

The principle of swarms is based on a natural phenomenon that is observed when a group of individual agents, each following a set of rules, display as a whole an emergent behaviour that could not be achieved based on the intelligence of an individual agent [1, 2]. In most naturally derived systems, the rules governing the agents are either properties of physics or evolved through time. In technical systems it is possible to define the rule set each agent follows to influence the emergent behavior of the system. However, once the complexity of a system begins to increase predicting the rule set that produces the desired emergent behavior becomes difficult to impossible. The best solution to this limitation is to simulate the swarm with a given rule set.

A sufficiently complex system is a multi-Unmanned Aerial Vehicle (UAV) Search and Rescue (SAR). SAR is currently conducted with human pilots in carefully choreographed search patterns that have remained relatively unchanged since they were formally introduced in 1956 [3]. SAR swarms have been simulated in previous work [4–6] with varying levels of simulation sophistication. By comparing the simulation conducted by Sammons [4] to the simulation conducted in this research, on a more sophisticated simulator, this paper begins to explore the effects of differing simulations with the same rule sets on the observed emergent behaviour.

2 Methodology

2.1 Experimental Set Up

This experiment is conducted using the UNSW Flight Gear Cluster Simulator (FGCS). The FGCS is an eleven computers simulator, pictured in Fig. 1, with eight computers dedicated to simulating the UAVs.

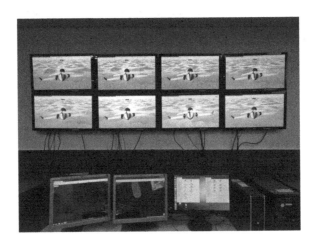

Fig. 1. The flight gear cluster simulator simulating a search and rescue operation with eight UAVs

Each computer is running Linux distribution Ubuntu version 12.04, have AMD Phenom II X2 555 central processing units and Nvidia GeForce GTX550Ti graphics processing units. The simulation runs the community driven, open source flight simulator software, Flightgear version 2.6.0. Flightgear is used in a number of research projects due to the accurate flight dynamics [7, 8], which are based on one of three different flight dynamics models used to determine how the UAVs fly.

For the experiment, the FGCS is set up to act as a decentralised swarm, where each UAV broadcasts its altitude, latitude, longitude and velocity only. By allowing UAVs to broadcast and receive only this limited information transfer, the need for UAVs to wait for commands is eliminated. However, lack of communication forces the UAVs to solve two problems that are normally solved by having a centralised controller. Firstly, the UAVs have to ensure that they avoid collisions with other UAVs; this may involve deviating from the selected optimal route. Secondly each UAV has to store its own map of the search area and update it as each member of the swarm searches an area.

Search Area. The search area is defined over a section of ocean and assumed to contain no waves or anomalies. Search objects are assumed to sit on the surface of the ocean allowing the search area to be considered two dimensional. This assumption applies only to the search area and does not affect the ability of the UAVs to fly at different altitudes.

A standard search area size is defined by the Australian Maritime Safety Authority (AMSA) [9], as approximately 40 nautical miles by 40 nautical miles for a parallel track search. This size allows the search to continue for a reasonable period of time, ensuring that the swarm behaviour can be observed, and therefore is selected for these experiments. The search area is divided up into a grid of 200 by 200, so that the probability of a search object existing at each position can be discretely distributed over it. The probability distribution is selected to be a Gaussian distribution, to align with previous research [4]. The Gaussian provides a prediction of where the search object is likely to be, with the centre being the most likely and the edges the least.

To perform the search, the UAVs utilise a greedy search algorithm with a limited lookahead, over the Gaussian distribution. The greedy search looks for the area of highest probability and directs the UAV in towards it. And by utilising a limited lookahead, the UAVs are prevented from always heading to exactly same point in the search area.

UAV. While the limited lookahead is performed on the probability distribution it is unrelated to what the UAV can actually see. To determine how far the UAV can see, the visible area is defined as function of altitude h, in metres, and the UAVs field of view FOV, which is detailed below.

$$s = \frac{1}{2}\left[\frac{2 \cdot h \cdot \tan\left(\frac{FOV}{2}\right)}{R_e \cdot \sin(I_G)}\right] \tag{1}$$

Where I_G is the grid increment in radians of latitude or longitude and R_e is the radius of the earth. When rounded, this equation gives the number of spaces s that the UAV can see in one direction from its position. The UAV being able to see an area does not guarantee that the search object will be found. The Gaussian distribution is updated as the UAV passes over a section of the grid, based on the altitude and velocity of the UAV, decreasing the probability that the search object will be found in that grid space. The following equation shows how the probability of a single grid space P_n decreases as a UAV views it.

$$P_n = \begin{cases} P_r & , \quad s = 6 \\ \frac{1}{10}\left[\frac{|i|+|j|}{0} + s\right] \cdot P_r, & s \geq 1 \\ 0 & , \quad s = 0 \end{cases} \tag{2}$$

Where i and j are the distance from the UAV in the x and y directions and P_r is the initial probability of the space in the distribution.

As Eqs. 1 and 2 show, at a low altitude (where s is 0) the probability of the grid space goes to zero as the UAV passes over, however only a single grid space can be viewed at a time. At higher altitudes more grid spaces may be viewed at one time, however the probability is reduced by a factor and does not reach zero. It is notable that the velocity of the UAV is not taken into account in these equations. This is because the calculations occur at every time-step and therefore the probability reduces multiple times for a single passover, the number of times is determined by the UAVs velocity.

These equations limit the minimum useful altitude to 200ft where only a single grid space can be seen and the maximum to 3000ft above which viewing the outermost grid spaces does not change their probability. These altitudes correspond to the minimum and maximum altitudes specified in the AMSA guidelines for search and rescue [9]. For these simulations the altitude for search is selected as approximately 2000ft and the velocity at 120 knots. These values allow for a reasonable view area and a relatively slow velocity. That the specified altitude and velocity are approximate rather than exact, is a side effect of using a realistic simulator.

2.2   Experimental Method

Two experiments are conducted in this research, with the first being an observation of the emergent behaviour of the swarm with differing numbers of agents and different starting positions. Each test in the experiment is run for fifteen minutes with the paths of the UAVs recorded and changes in the probability distribution monitored.

The second experiment is a direct comparison to the work conducted by Sammons [4] on the Netlogo simulator; with the same set up, starting positions and number of agents. Again, the UAV paths and changes to the probability distribution are recorded. In this experiment however, the test is run only until the UAVs have completed their first manoeuvre to better match the experiments run by Sammons [4].

Both experiments are qualitative comparisons of the paths taken by each UAV. To make this comparison, each UAV records and stores its path using its flight data recorder. The data is then plotted on a map of the search area for comparison.

3 Results

3.1 Experiment One

Through changing starting positions and numbers of UAVs for each test, Experiment One looks at the behaviour of the UAVs to determine if any emergent behaviour is displayed.

The routes taken by the two UAVs in different starting positions is shown in Fig. 2, with test three on the top left and test four on the top right. While the routes taken when the number of UAVs is changed is shown in Fig. 2, with test five on the bottom left and test six on the bottom right.

When looking at the paths taken by the UAVs it is difficult to discern any emergent behaviour. There are some clear individual behaviours; UAVs that start in the centre of the starting edge appear to search the North and South of the search area more than the UAVs starting on the sides, which search more to the East and West. These are behaviours of the individual however and not that of the swarm.

When looking at specific snapshots during the experiment an emergent behaviour is apparent. Regularly during the simulation, the UAVs come together as if as a flock. This behaviour is shown in Fig. 3, with the image on the left, from test seven, showing a flock which would be expected to be seen in migrating birds. The image on the right shows similar behaviour, observed in test ten with all eight UAVs. In the right-hand image, the flock is not as well defined, but it is interesting to see that this behaviour occurs with the two UAVs towards the bottom left as well as with the main group.

This behaviour can be explained in one of two ways. The first explanation is that the UAVs are following the path that they would take with or without the nearby UAVs presence. The lead UAV follows the path of highest probability, hence decreasing the probability along that path. For the following UAVs the path of highest probability is just offset from the lead UAVs path, where the probability is still unchanged.

The second explanation is that the UAVs just behind the lead UAV are able to see ahead of the lead UAV and head towards the high probability. This high value then changes as the lead UAV reaches it, causing the following UAV to turn towards the next highest probability, again just in front of the lead UAV. The first explanation appears to be more likely based on how closely previous UAV paths are followed in most cases, shown in Fig. 2. However, given how common this emergent behaviour is, the second explanation appears to be more likely.

In either case the behaviour only occurs near the centre of the search area, towards the area of most probability, once the UAVs pass into the area of lower probability they disperse in different directions. This could be due to the lack of uniformity in the probability distribution in this region, or because the UAVs are avoiding the edge of the search area.

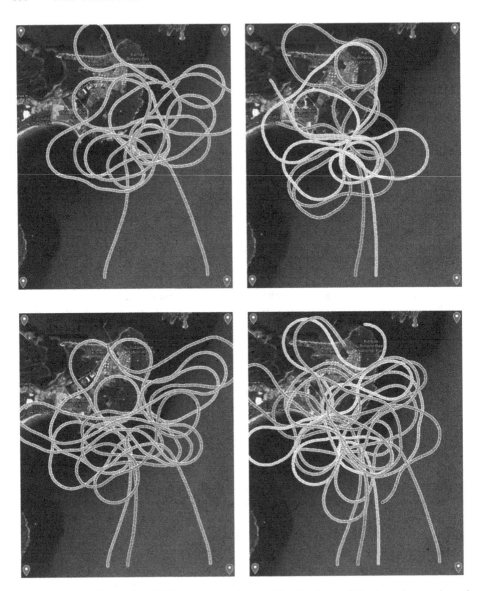

Fig. 2. Paths followed by UAVs as the starting position is changed (top) or the number of UAVs changed (bottom).

3.2   Experiment Two

The second experiment is set up to compare to the FGCS results to the results of Sammons [4] using the Netlogo simulator. The tests are run with the same number of UAVs, starting from the same position, and run until the UAVs have completed their first manoeuvre.

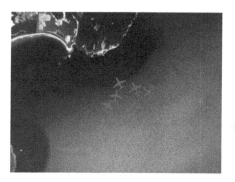 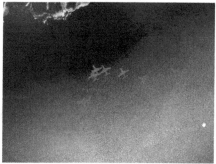

Fig. 3. The flocking behaviour shown by the UAVs is an interesting emergent behaviour of the UAV swarm, which occurs regularly during the experiments. The left image shows five UAVs in a near perfect flocking formation, while the image on the right shows that flocking can occur with a large group of UAVs or between just two.

Test One. The UAVs in test one, Fig. 4, show almost identical behaviour to what is seen on Netlogo, with both UAVs converging together towards the centre before turning off in opposite directions.

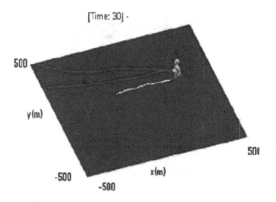 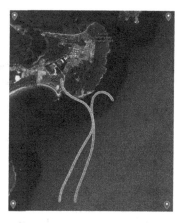

Fig. 4. Test one. The Netlogo simulation by sammons [4] on the left and the FGCS simulation on the right. The UAVs in both experiments follow similar paths. Image on the left courtesy of Sammons [4].

Test Two. The UAVs in test two again follow similar paths to the paths observed in Sammons' experiment, Fig. 5. However, in Sammons' experiment two of the three UAVs converge together with the last one staying separate, where on the FGCS all the UAVs converge together before turning outwards. This is could be because of slightly different probability distributions used in each simulation or it could be as a result of the different physics models used by the simulators.

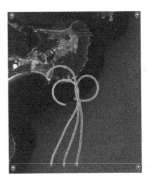

Fig. 5. Test two. The paths followed by the UAVs on the FGCS in test two (right) are again similar to the paths followed by the Netlogo simulation (left), with the manoeuvre loops appearing smaller on the Netlogo simulation. Image on the left courtesy of Sammons [4].

Test Three. In test three, Fig. 6, it becomes more difficult to say if the results of Sammons are similar or not. In both experiments the UAVs are showing the same inclination to start turning slightly after passing the centre of the search area. However, it seems that the convergence of the UAVs on the FGCS is affecting their similarity to the Sammons' experiment where the UAVs stay comparatively separate.

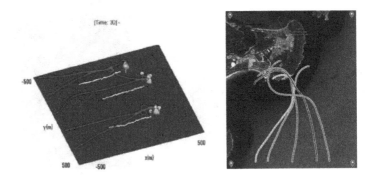

Fig. 6. Test Three. The UAV paths followed in test three (right) is similar to the paths followed in Sammons' experiment (left) in their tendency to turn after the centre of the search area. However, the UAVs on the FGCS have a much greater tendency to converge to the centre. Image on the left courtesy of Sammons [4].

4 Discussion

The results outlined in the above section show a developed swarm displaying emergent behaviour. The resultant search pattern is non optimal as the UAVs have to pass over pre-searched areas in order to reach areas of higher probability.

The results have similarities to those produced by Sammons [4], however they are not exactly the same. Tests one and two of experiment two, are almost identical to

Sammons' experiments, which contrasts with test three which bears only a small resemblance to the corresponding experiment. Swarms are complex, and it is difficult to say if the differences are due to variations between the models and probability distributions used, or to do with the more realistic physics models used in the FGCS. To determine the true cause of the differences, the simulations need to be set up and tested quantitatively on both simulators. This is outside the scope and timeline of this paper; however, the results confirm that predicting the emergent behaviour of a swarm based on a rule model is very difficult.

The flocking emergent behaviour displayed by the swarm is an interesting emergent behaviour. It not something that the swarm has been programmed to do, yet it occurs regularly during the simulation, with at least a portion of the UAVs. Previously, this behaviour has been intentionally created through a rule set on the FGCS by Shawn Goh [10], as part of a thesis topic at UNSW. That this behaviour appears unintentionally as part of SAR is surprising. The cause of this behaviour is not currently clear, however it is likely to be either an artefact of the highest probability points being next to each other or an effect of the probability changing due to the leading UAV.

5 Conclusion

Obtaining a specific emergent behaviour from a swarm is a complex problem, as the desired behaviour cannot be directly specified. The only method of controlling the behaviour is through the use of a rule set or rule model. Simulations of swarms are run to show that the emergent behaviour is consistent with the desired behaviour. For search and rescue swarms, examined using approximate models, there remains the question of the limitations of the approximations. In this work, SAR UAVs are modelled using a flight simulator that uses a number of physics models to provide realistic flight dynamics and hence realistic search patterns.

This work performs a SAR simulation using a greedy search with limited lookahead, this rule set produced an emergent behaviour, in the form of flocking of the UAVs, almost identical to the flight behaviour of a flock of birds. The SAR swarm flight paths are qualitatively similar to those calculated by Sammons [4], who employed Netlogo a less realistic UAV simulator with no dynamics physics. The main difference between the two experiments is that the UAVs on the flight gear cluster simulator tend to head towards the centre of the search area more quickly than on Netlogo. This is either caused by differences in the experimental set up or by the extra realism provided the FGCS. Future quantitative research can be used to determine which factor or factors may have caused the differences.

6 Future Works

The results of this work lead directly towards two areas of research. The first is a continuation of the research outlined in this paper. The research in this paper is a qualitative analysis of the emergent behaviour between different simulators, the next stage of this is to perform quantitative research. This can be completed by either recreating SAR on another simulator such as Netlogo, as used by Sammons, or by comparing the emergent behaviour from the other rule model used by Sammons. The other rule model has been used in a quantitative experiment so the results can be easily compared. Furthermore, this model appears to produce far better coverage of the search area than the greedy search with limited lookahead.

This rule model is still a greedy search with limited lookahead. However, instead of looking for the highest probability point the UAV looks for the highest probability path. This is a simple change to the current algorithm where instead of looking for the highest probability that can be seen, the integral of each possible path is taken with respect to time, as below, and the highest probability path taken.

$$Pr_{path} = \int_{t_c}^{t_s} Pr \, dt \qquad (3)$$

Where P_r is the probability at each point on the path, t_c is the current time, t_s is the total time steps at the end of the path and Pr_{path} is the probability of the whole path, which is aimed to be maximised. As the probability distribution is discrete, the integral can Instead be taken as a summation.

$$Pr_{path} = \sum_{i=1}^{t_s} Pr_i \qquad (4)$$

Here Pr_i is the probability in each grid in the path, and i begins at one as zero is taken to be the position of the UAV.

The second area of research that follows directly from this paper, is to investigate whether allowing the swarm to determine its own rule set through machine learning, produces a more effective search pattern than is currently used in SAR or research. The framework of the program has been set up so that the implementation of a learning algorithm is simple to do.

References

1. Krause, J., Ruxton, G.D., Krause, S.: Swarm intelligence in animals and humans. Trends in Ecol. Evol. **25**(1), 28–34 (2010)
2. Bonabeau, E., Marco, D., Theraulaz, G.: Swarm Intelligence: From Natural to Artificial Systems, vol. 1. Oxford University Press, Oxford (1999)
3. Koopman, B.O.: The theory of search. ii. target detection. Oper. Res. **4**(5), 503–531 (1956)
4. Sammons, P.J.: Development of a System in the Loop Simulator for the Control of Multiple Autonomous Unmanned Aircraft. University of New South Wales, Syndey (2011)
5. Rahmes, M., Chester, D., Hunt, J., Chiasson, B.: Optimizing cooperative cognitive search and rescue UAVS. In: Autonomous Systems: Sensors, Vehicles, Security, and the Internet of Everything. vol. 10643, p. 106430T. International Society for Optics and Photonics (2018)
6. Arbeit, A.: Adaptation and Automation of Search and Rescue Patterns with Implementation for an Operational Unmanned Aircraft System. Ph.D thesis (2014)
7. Perry, A.R.: The flightgear flight simulator. In: Proceedings of the USENIX Annual Technical Conference (2004)

8. Sorton, E., Hammaker, S.: Simulated flight testing of an autonomous unmanned aerial vehicle using flightgear. In: Infotech@ Aerospace, p. 7083 (2005)
9. Australian Maritime Safety Authority: National Search and Rescue Manual (February 2018)
10. Goh, S.: Development of Possible Military UAV Swarm Applications. University of New South Wales, Syndey (2012)

Simulating Search and Rescue Operations Using Swarm Technology to Determine How Many Searchers Are Needed to Locate Missing Persons/Objects in the Shortest Time

John Page, Robert Armstrong, and Faqihza Mukhlish$^{(\boxtimes)}$ (iD)

The University of New South Wales, Sydney, NSW, Australia
f.mukhlish@student.unsw.edu.au

Abstract. The use of multiple computer-based agents formed into a swarm has found potential applications in a number of tasks [1]. Because of its flexibility and scalability, by using collaborative behavior [2], a swarm system is able to complete tasks. One area that is of particular interest is the usage of a swarm system in the search element of search and rescue missions [3]. The success of a search mission depends on the deployment of a number of assets and as human driven assets are not only expensive, in severe conditions, they can put the operators at risk. Hence, utilising unmanned autonomous assets such as swarms is preferable for future developments. However, as the cost of the autonomous assets is relatively low, a question arises as to how many agents the swarm should be composed of. Little work has been done in this area with the assumption being made that the more assets the better. Thus, the aim of this research is to investigate, through simulation, the effects the number of agents has on the need for information.

Keywords: Swarm · Drone · Unmanned aerial vehicle · Search and rescue · Search pattern · Rescue operations

1 Introduction

Search and rescue techniques are well known and have been used extensively and successfully for many different missions. However, these usually operate with a small number of agents due to available assets. This creates a problem as a considerable amount of information is required to complete the mission in the shortest amount of time and thus maximise survivability.

With the introduction of swarm robotics into search and rescue missions, they can now deploy a much larger number of search assets. However, the impact of increased assets' availability needs to be investigated to ensure the maximum benefit is generated from the increased number of agents available. Thus, the effect that the number of agents in a swarm has on its performance is examined in this article. This is important because swarms consist of distributed, relatively simple intelligent agents that when combined a group intelligence emerges. This emergent intelligence is often unpredictable, and the process is often disruptive. In this article, a swarm of unmanned aerial

© Springer Nature Singapore Pte Ltd. 2019
A. Naweed et al. (Eds.): ASC 2019, CCIS 1067, pp. 106–112, 2019.
https://doi.org/10.1007/978-981-32-9582-7_8

vehicles is used to conduct a search and rescue mission. Drones can undertake various standard searches but may have limitations due to available intelligence and restricted sensor capability. As such it is un-determined what advantages this approach will generate. Some obvious issues that need to be investigated given that swarms generate a collective or emergent intelligence using relatively limited distributed intelligence are: How smart do agents need to be if you have enough of them? Is there a point where agents no longer need to be so smart? How intelligent does the overall rescue operation need to be in order for the information required to be generated and how does this relate to the numbers deployed? Hence, to answer these questions, several investigations are demonstrated in this article to examine the relationship between intelligent levels and number of agents.

The aim of this paper is to look at what effect the number of agents participating has on a search and rescue mission. This is done through simulation which is a way to investigate swarms with various potential searches and rescue operations safely.

2   Search Methods

There are a number of search strategies outlined in the National Search and Rescue Manual [4]. These search methods are the standard for search strategies around the world, and by and large have remained unchanged for years. For this paper six were considered. Creep, Parallel, Square, Random, Weighted Random and Greedy.

2.1   Creep and Parallel Search

This is a fairly common method of search which can be modified as shown Fig. 1. If the path of the lost vehicle is well known, then a creep search is preferred. If it is believed the track may have deviated, a parallel search may be used.

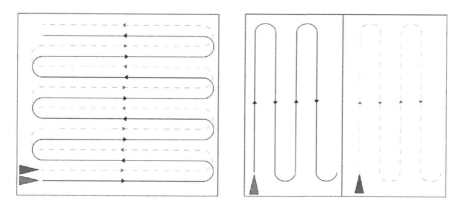

Fig. 1. Creep (left) and Parallel (right) search 2 agents

2.2 Square Search

If the initial location of the event is well defined, but there is little additional information, then a square search is often the best strategy adopted. The starting point of the search is the area with highest probability. Then, the search takes square-shaped lines to cover the area around the starting point. The expanding square shape is applied to search for victims that have moved from the initial location (Fig. 2).

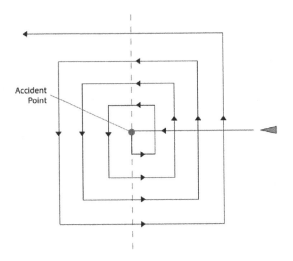

Fig. 2. A square search

2.3 Random Search

Simply searches a space randomly ignoring the areas already searched.

2.4 Weighted Random Search

A weighted random search is an improvement on the random search that biases the selected location based on other information that may be available such as wind, currents and most likely location of the initial situation.

2.5 Greedy Search

The greedy search uses probability to maximise the chance of locating the victim. A Bayesian type probability map is constructed by using experience or a selected prior distribution, and the agents search out the distribution from the highest point to the lower probability areas. Theoretically, this should provide the best outcome because it takes into account all the available data from past and current events. But, in practice, it is very sensitive to data error and an ill-selected prior probability. Note for this simulation greedy is given accurate information to test it as a well-informed search, the only searches that are incorrectly informed are; parallel, creep and square (Fig. 3).

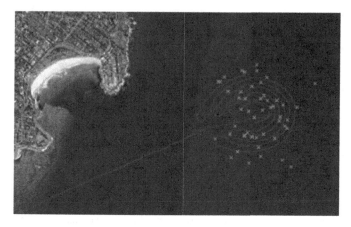

Fig. 3. Typical result of a greedy search [5]

3   Simulation

In order to investigate and compare the six methods, simulation was used. A number of simulations were carried out with each method using various numbers of agents, search widths and placements distributions for the people. Anylogic© was used as the simulation platform which is a commercial product able to model using dynamic modelling, event modelling and particle modelling [6]. For this work particle modelling was used. The average time before a person was detected was determined for thirty runs using a set number of agents and averaged. This was repeated with a different number of agents for a total of thirty cases.

3.1   Beach

The area in which the simulation was run is defined as the beach. For this simulation the scale was set to one pixel being equivalent to one metre.

Fig. 4. Beach during a random search run [7] (Color figure online)

Figure 4 shows the beach which is the working area of the simulation during a run of the random strategy. The red area is that already explored while the light blue is that waiting to be explored.

4   Results

The results were plotted in a number of ways and for each run, the results followed a similar form. From Fig. 5, we can see that the greedy search reached a high level of success quickly and continued to improve until about nine agents were deployed. The weighted random followed a similar trajectory but did not do as well as the greedy search. The success of weighted random search closely following greedy is unexpected as it was not expected to approach the success of greedy search as fast as it did.

The parallel and the creep strategies perform about as well as each other. These two search methods are the most effective for searching for a person who is expected to be placed in a random distribution.

The square search is the least effective of the methods graphed, again as one might have expected as it is incorrectly told to expect the person to be at the centre of the area, so tends to spend most time at the centre rather than searching the entire area evenly.

The plotting of the random is not visible in this result as it is indistinguishable from weighted random search in this case.

What this shows is that for the size of the search area defined, after about 11 drones the amount of information becomes irrelevant.

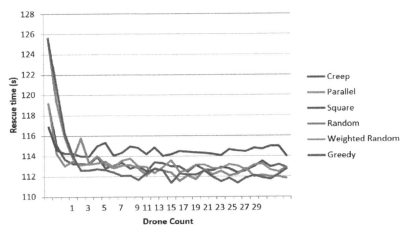

Fig. 5. Typical results from simulation with a random distribution for the person [7]

Another feature of this graph is the greedy swarm, seems to improve up to about nine agents, which agrees closely with some inhouse research. The Weighted Random swarm may improve a little with a further two agents before the noise takes over.

The square search does not seem to improve much beyond, a swarm of three agents. This however is a limitation of the simulation because of the size of the search area. The complexity of the search algorithm begins to increase rapidly at this agent count. So greedy search is used as an intelligent search at higher numbers of agents.

When the area to be searched is increased the number of agents to minimise the time does increase but not as much as one might have expected. The basic pattern however remains the same. This introduces the idea that it is more efficient to search large areas with higher drone counts. This could lead to a massive change in search and rescue methods, as the requirement to gather large amounts of information to reduce the search area may not be necessary (Fig. 6).

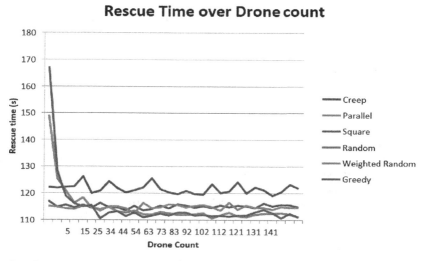

Fig. 6. Effect of a significantly increase search area for a random distribution of the person [7]

5   Conclusion

The simulation results follow the trend that might be expected, however it shows that the speed and efficiency may not be to expectation. One point of interest is the possibility that search and rescue could be split between; over saturated search strategies, where you use the agents to search areas where the number of agents exceeds the point of convergence; and under saturated search strategies, which are the more traditional search methods. The minimisation of the time taken to locate the lost person being hunted, particularly in an ocean or other exposed location is vital to their survival. The results indicate that the more information available, the better the outcome, for small number of agents. However this assumes the data is sound, and this limitation seems to disappear if you are able to reach the number of agents, where the results seem to converge. In the case of the greedy search for example the probability is built into a Bayesian map. The location of the victim was then selected based on a scholastic search of the space. This implies that the information the probability map is based on is completely accurate both in terms of the variables selected and the values attached to them. In a real-world situation this is unlikely to be the case and any errors might be very significant. To overcome this, it would make sense to use a heterogeneous rather than a homogeneous swarm with individual agents adopting different strategies in a situation where the number of agents is limited; this would be a useful area of future research.

Another area that we is currently being researched is having one or more of the agents human controlled. These humans would not direct the swarm but act as an element of it. The advantage of such a system is that while computer-based systems by-and-large outperform humans when sufficient data is available, they find it hard to make a decision on limited data where humans do rather better. Many successful rescues have resulted from human intuition and it is hard to build hunches into AI.

Another area of interest is looking at the possibility and effectiveness of search methods where the swarm searches in a normal search method using the information provided, but tells the agents to search in smaller search areas using where the agents are oversaturated and can search randomly.

References

1. Şahin, E.: Swarm robotics: from sources of inspiration to domains of application. In: Şahin, E., Spears, W.M. (eds.) SR 2004. LNCS, vol. 3342, pp. 10–20. Springer, Heidelberg (2005). https://doi.org/10.1007/978-3-540-30552-1_2
2. Brambilla, M., Ferrante, E., Birattari, M., Dorigo, M.: Swarm robotics: a review from the swarm engineering perspective. Swarm Intell. 7(1), 1–41 (2013)
3. Mukhlish, F., Page, J., Bain, M.: Reward-based evolutionary swarm UAVs on search and rescue mission. In: AEROSPACE - 18th Australian International Aerospace Congress, Melbourne, Australia, pp. 348–353 (2019)
4. Stone, T. (ed.): National Search and Rescue Manual, 1st edn. Australian Maritime Safety Authority (AMSA), Canbera (2018)
5. Sammon, P.J., Page, J.: Experimentation and validation of vehicle cluster simulator using NetLogo, Adelaide, SA, Australia (2009)
6. AnyLogic: Simulation Modeling Software Tools & Solutions for Business. https://www.anylogic.com/. Accessed 29 May 2019
7. Armstrong, R.: Effect the size of a swarm has on search and rescue performance. Bachelor of Engineering, University of New South Wales, New South Wales, Australia (2018)

Defence-Oriented Technology and Training

Balancing Defence Service Experience and Technical Skills to Deliver Simulation Workforce Capability: A Case Study

Karen Louise Blackmore[1]([⊠]) [iD] and Evan William Henry Allitt[2]

[1] School of Electrical Engineering and Computing, The University of Newcastle, Callaghan, Australia
karen.blackmore@newcastle.edu.au
[2] Cubic Defence Australia, Fyshwick, ACT, Australia

Abstract. Delivering the external workforce to assist in providing simulation capability within the Australian Defence Force (ADF) is a complex task. In particular, securing, training, and retaining personnel with requisite technical skills to deliver distributed simulation environments, paired with detailed understanding of Defence systems and processes, is a growing problem. These issues are further complicated in the provision of contract simulation workforce, where career progression opportunities and long-term workforce security impose additional constraints. In this work, we examine the technical and service experience, as well as the qualifications and training, of the workforce within Cubic Defence Australia, a key simulation workforce provider to the ADF. This analysis serves to highlight some of the unique issues facing the provision of the Defence simulation workforce. Further, we identify the experience sets of this workforce, and consider the relationships between prior service, training, and education, and employment success within Cubic. From our analysis, we also provide a discussion of the transferability of similar or aligned skillsets from other roles areas to these simulation roles, providing direction on the potential future sustainability and growth of the workforce.

Keywords: Simulation · Competencies · Workforce · Education · Training · Case study

1 Introduction

The use of simulation systems in training contexts has seen significant growth [1, 2]. This growth has been largely driven by increased computing power [3], although a number of other factors can reasonably be considered to have combined to fuel this growth. This includes symbiotic developments in the availability and capability of training system content development platforms, born largely through advances in the game development industry. Together, these advances fuel the realisation of the practical and cost benefits associated with the use of virtual simulation training platforms [4]. In effect, simulation-based training has the ability to deliver training outcomes at reduced cost, reduced risk to participants, training assets, and environments, and potentially, in areas where other forms of training targeting the same learning

© Springer Nature Singapore Pte Ltd. 2019
A. Naweed et al. (Eds.): ASC 2019, CCIS 1067, pp. 115–128, 2019.
https://doi.org/10.1007/978-981-32-9582-7_9

outcomes would be impractical. This is often true for large distributed training exercises such as those commonly seen in the defence and military contexts.

The resource requirements underpinning the delivery of simulation training systems is expanding. Significant technological skills are required where simulation training systems are tasked with delivering dynamic, distributed training environments and virtual assets to multiple stakeholders. In these instances, the requirements gathering and system delivery to meet these requirements is complicated by the differing expectations and norms for different stakeholder groups. This is further complicated, in defence and military contexts, where these norms and operating models are often entrenched in deep structures and organisational rules. Thus, navigating the rapidly changing technology and the intricacies of the defence landscape to deliver these simulation systems requires a highly skilled and knowledgeable simulation workforce.

Within the Australian Defence Force (ADF), simulation capability is delivered through a combination of ADF personnel and external contract workforce. The internal workforce is distributed across the different service operations of Defence, with many roles associated with niche, single service, training operations [5]. Where simulation is required to deliver combined training across the three arms of the ADF (i.e. Army, Navy, and Air Force), or indeed in partnership with other allied forces, the external contract workforce plays a pivotal role. The external workforce is largely comprised of Defence veterans who are able to use their extensive service training and experience to translate and facilitate the establishment of system requirements, and the delivery of the technological solution to meet these requirements. In this role, they work closely with non-defence cognate workforce members who generally fill roles requiring a higher level of technical acumen.

This combination of Defence veterans and non-defence cognate employees is currently delivering Defence simulation training capability. However, a number of issues emerge that may impact on the sustainability and growth of this workforce provision. In the first instance, the dependence on Defence veterans with sufficient technical acumen to fill the professional interactor roles is constrained. There is no specific pipeline within Defence for attracting and retaining these individuals to the external contractor workforce, creating a competitive employment marketplace. Secondly, the roles filled by the non-defence cognate employees may lay outside of traditional information and communication technology (ICT) position descriptions, creating ambiguity amongst this subset of the workforce. Although these issues appear obvious, there is little existing work that explores the impact that these issues have on the existing workforce, and thus no clear strategies for developing current and future simulation training capability.

In this work, we consider a case study of a large external workforce contract supplier to the ADF, Cubic Defence Australia [6]. This study focusses on the analysis of the educational backgrounds of employees of this simulation workforce provider. We identify the experience sets of this workforce, and consider the relationships between prior service, training, and education, and employment success within Cubic. From our analysis, we also provide direction on strategies for the potential future sustainability and growth of the workforce. However, we begin by first providing some background to the study that includes consideration of the broader modelling and simulation (M&S) field, and the existing pathways for professionals within this general field to gain the necessary skills to fulfil simulation roles.

2 Background

A simulation is a representation of an object or system in the real world. This representation frequently aims to allow for exploration of the behaviour of a system, to optimise the functioning of the system, or to act as a prompt or environment for considering human behavior [7]. These different simulation aims result in approaches that range from mathematical models of systems with relationships expressed as mathematical functions (constructive simulations), computer based virtual environments where one or more human participants engage in simulated scenarios or vice versa (virtual simulations), to real people interacting with real systems (live simulations). The Live, Virtual, Constructive (LVC) classification is the dominant framework for describing simulation in the defence or military domain [8]. Within this framework, simulations are used in variety of application areas including analysis, research and development (R&D), test and evaluation, and training [8]. From a defence perspective, the LVC classification framework provides a coherent overview of the ways in which simulation supports and enhances capabilities (Fig. 1).

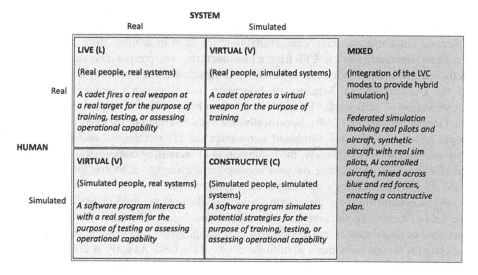

Fig. 1. Simulation classification framework adapted from Hodson and Baldwin (2009).

Evolving requirements and expectations for simulation in defence contexts has given rise to a new 'mixed' (M) mode in the LVC framework (LVC-M). The mixed mode combines traditional live, virtual, and constructive paradigms into a single, often distributed, approach to delivering training capability [9, 10]. Ready access to new commercial off the shelf (COTS) virtual and augmented reality head mounted displays

(HMDs) act as a significant enabler of the mixed approach [11]. However, the real focus of mixed reality simulation lies in integrating multiple entities of differing levels of realism and fidelity into rich simulation environments [10]. While these entities may be located in the live, virtual, or constructive space, applications are increasingly calling for the combining of large numbers of distributed entities into federated simulation environments.

Federated simulation manages the complexity of systems integration through distributed yet parallel design, development, and analysis of subsystems [12]. Within the ADF, sophisticated training platforms support capability sustainment and development across the LVC training framework within Army, Navy and Air Force. Increasingly, these systems are being integrated to "provide a joint synthetic training environment for training crews in mission rehearsals and tactics evaluation" [13; p. 1]. From a technical perspective, this integration relies on advanced distributed simulation, voice communications, data link, simulation fidelity, networking, and encryption to achieve an effective federated synthetic environment. From a management perspective, achieving coordinated interaction amongst disparate systems to achieve a common view or "common operating picture" presents challenges that draw heavily on softer skills [14].

The emergence of federated simulation systems occurs in tandem to more general developments in the area of Cyber-Physical Systems. CPS "are integrations of computation with physical processes. Embedded computers and networks monitor and control the physical processes, usually with feedback loops where physical processes affect computations and vice versa." [15; p. 363]. While no specific studies that examined the competences required for the design and deployment of large-scale federated simulation systems were available at the time of writing, there are insights available from early work in CPS from a manufacturing perspective. One such example is the identification of competence needs by Dworschak and Zaiser [16] from analysis of the German Federal Ministry of Education and Research's initiative for early identification of skill needs (FreQueNz) and the Office of Technology Assessment at the German Bundestag (TAB). Specifically, the authors highlight the need for more in-depth technical skills and combined knowledge on IT, electronics, and mechanical systems" (p. 348). Additionally, the combination of increasing complexity, geographic distribution, and dependence on tacit knowledge are seen as a source for increasing need for interdisciplinary (including social) competence.

As is evident from the discussion above, the skillsets required of professionals in the field of modelling and simulation continue to evolve. Additionally, the demand for qualified professionals in this field is also increasing, giving rise to some concern over capacity for skilled individuals to fulfil the needs of the field. As early as 2000, calls for an urgent response to the growing demand for simulation professionals were made [2, 17]. In order to address these shortfalls, some work to identify the broad set of skills required for simulation professionals has been presented [18, 19]. A key example of this can be found in the work of Kincaid and Westerlund [3], where a taxonomy of the knowledge and skills required of simulation professionals was presented (Table 1).

While providing a relevant overview of the disciplinary breadth and diversity of simulation professional roles, the framework is not comprehensive. In particular, it does not address the complexity of tasks involved in the implementation and delivery of more complex simulation systems that were eluded to in the earlier discussion of

Table 1. Taxonomy of M&S professional knowledge

	Topic	Simulation model developer	Scientist/Experimenter	Instructional simulation developer
Math & Physics	Numerical Analysis	Low	High	Medium
	Statistics	Medium	High	Medium
	Linear Algebra		Medium	
	Differential Equations	Low	Medium	Low
	Dynamics		Low	
	Electric Circuits		Low	
Industrial Engineering	Programming	Low	High	Low
	Nonlinear Optimization	Low	High	
	Sensitivity Analysis	Low	High	
	Cost Models	Medium	Low	Low
Human Factors	User Interface Design	High	High	High
	Training Theory	Medium	High	High
	Usability Testing			High
Software Engineering	Modular Program Design	High	High	
	Verification & Validation	High		Medium
	Testing	High	Low	Medium
	Metrics	High		
Computer Science	Database Systems	High	Medium	
	Operating Systems	High	Medium	
	Computer Networks	High	Low	
	Distributed Systems	High	Low	Low
	Artificial Intelligence	Medium	Low	

(continued)

Table 1. (*continued*)

	Topic	Simulation model developer	Scientist/Experimenter	Instructional simulation developer
Instructional Technology	Instructional System Design			High
	Media Selection			High
	Task Analysis	Medium		High
	Instructional Evaluation			High
	Learning Theory			High

Note. Reprinted from [3]

federated simulation systems and CPS. Here, proprietary system and tacit domain knowledge are crucial, and combine to make cross-sector evaluation of simulation systems, and the skills required to deliver these systems, difficult [20]. Given the evident difficulties in capturing the skills and knowledge for simulation professional roles, it stands to reason that there are many diverse pathways to simulation careers. From an educational perspective, the taxonomy provided by Kincaid and Westerlund [3] points to the role of vocational, undergraduate, and postgraduate programs in mathematics, physics, engineering, information technology, computer science, software engineering, psychology, and education. This can be further extended to consider recently relevant topic areas such as cyber security, computer gaming, advanced interfaces, virtual and augmented reality, and robotics. However, tacit domain knowledge is of noted importance in many simulation roles, and thus it is difficult to evaluate how domain experience impacts on career pathways and subsequent success in simulation roles.

From the perspective of the employer, the reliance on individuals with unique technical skills and in-depth domain knowledge is likely to create issues with attracting suitably qualified simulation professionals. Additionally, as many of the roles for simulation professionals lie within the information technology (IT) domain, it is probable that the known issue of high turnover amongst IT personnel [21, 22] will be experienced by employers.

We undertake a case study in order to shed some light on the role tacit knowledge in the career pathways and employment success of simulation professionals. In this case study, we examine the technical and service experience, as well as the qualifications and training, of the workforce within Cubic Defence Australia, a key simulation workforce provider to the ADF. In the following section, we provide a brief overview of the case study organisation. Following this, we present the results of exploratory and descriptive analysis of their simulation workforce.

3 Case Study - Organisation Overview

Cubic Corporation commenced operations in San Diego in 1951 and is now a NYSE listed company (CUB), with over $USD1.4B in market capitalisation and over 7,700 employees in over 50 countries. Cubic Corporation is, essentially, a technology company comprised of three technologically focused business units; Cubic Transportation Systems (CTS), Cubic Mission Solutions (CMS), and Cubic Global Defense (CGD).

CTS is the leading integrator of payment and information solutions and related services for intelligent travel applications in the transportation industry. CMS is Cubic's Computers, Intelligence, Surveillance and Reconnaissance (C4ISR) business which includes capabilities for military, intelligence, security and commercial missions. These C4ISR solutions provide information capture, assessment, exploitation and dissemination in a secure network-centric environment. Lastly, CGD is Cubic's training business unit and is a world leading provider of advanced military training services and simulation systems. While they deliver training at all levels and for a range of audiences, the primary focus is centred on identifying and rapidly integrating innovative technologies into military training systems and services to provide militaries around the world with cutting-edge means to ensure the operational readiness of their forces.

Cubic Defence Australia Pty Ltd (CDAus) is a subsidiary of CGD. CDAus has a number of contracts with the ADF to facilitate and/or deliver training, thus providing external simulation contract workforce to the ADF. In particular, they deliver specialist services in exercise planning and control, develop, design and deliver live instrumented simulation, and manage and deliver constructive and federated simulation services. In this case study we focus on the analysis of CDAus staff employed in technical constructive and federated simulation-based roles.

Cubic provides three different types of workforce into the different simulation environments in which it is engaged. One is largely Professional Interactor (PI) based; that is, staff who interact with military personnel (end users) to develop and plan the training exercise. Another group are the field and analytical staff who are largely engaged with live simulation systems, and the training data analysis that accompanies managing instrumented exercises in the field. The final group are those staff provisioning constructive and federated simulation support services; they plan and deliver the hardware infrastructure and the simulation software environment through which exercises are run and supported. As such, the roles, responsibilities and requirements of Cubic's constructive and federated simulation workforce vary significantly, depending on the environment, the customer, and contractual obligations.

4 Results

In total, data for 59 positions within 39 unique simulation position descriptions was obtained from Cubic for the case study (Table 2). Of these, all but six (6) roles were filled at the time of data collection (21 November 2018), leaving data for 53 employees included in this analysis. On average, these employees have 10+ years of experience recorded in their employment files.

Superficially, the majority of position descriptions are identical to those that might be expected in IT, computer science, or software engineering roles outside of the simulation field. Additionally, it should be noted that levels of seniority are implied in many of the position descriptions. For the purposes of this case study, position descriptions containing the words 'Lead', 'Senior', 'Manager', or 'Supervisor' are considered as Senior Roles.

Table 2. Simulation position descriptions and personnel numbers for CDAus technical constructive and federated simulation-based roles

Position descriptions	Number of positions	Number of filled positions
Administrator Network	5	5
Administrator Systems	7	7
Administrator Systems CGD	7	7
Assoc Terrain Developer	1	1
Developer Terrain	1	1
Engineer Information Security Senior	1	1
Engineer Systems Senior Defence	1	1
Helpdesk Tech	1	1
Info Tech	4	3
Information Technician ADSTC	1	1
Integration Tech	2	1
Lead Core Infrastructure	1	1
Lead Engineering	1	1
Lead Integration	1	1
Lead Sim & Training Networks	1	1
Lead Simulation	1	1
Lead Tech Projects	1	1
Linux Administrator	2	1
Manager Operational IT	1	1
Network Tech	4	4
Planner Exercise	1	1
Planner Exercise Senior	1	1
Sim Tech	3	3
Simulation Principal Lead	1	1
Snr Program Manager	1	1
Supervisor Systems Admin	2	2
System Engineer	1	0
System Security Officer	1	0
Systems Manager	1	1
Tech Exercise Planner	1	1
Technical Writer	1	0
Terrain Developer	1	1
Grand Total	59	53

In total, 20 of the 53 (32%) positions are currently filled by employees who are ADF veterans (Ex-ADF), leaving 68% of the workforce with a non-ADF background. In order to consider whether the tacit Defence knowledge of veterans results in simulation career advantage, we consider the proportional distribution of Ex-ADF and non-ADF employees across senior and other roles (Table 3). These results clearly demonstrate the increased likelihood that Ex-ADF staff will occupy senior simulation roles, with 60% of the Ex-ADF occupying senior roles within the organisation. Additionally, of the 52 employees with years of experience recorded in their employment files, Ex-ADF veterans average 13+ years compared to 10+ years for non-ADF, which also may account for differences in role seniority. However, no detail on how relevant the years of experience are to the immediate role being performed are provided.

Table 3. Proportion of senior and other roles filled by Ex-ADF and Non-ADF staff

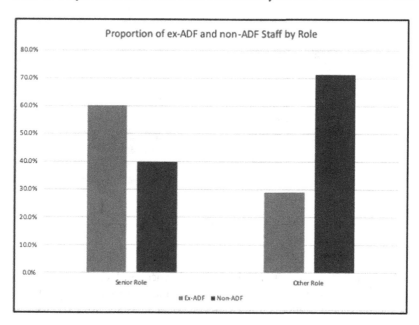

As previously discussed, tacit domain knowledge, while notably important, must be paired with sufficient technical skills to perform required simulation roles. We thus next consider the educational backgrounds of Ex-ADF and Non-ADF employees (Table 4). Interestingly, both groups have a similar number of individuals with bachelor's degree level qualifications, at 35% and 36% for Ex-ADF and Non-ADF employees respectively. However, if we consider those staff with master's level qualifications, 40% of Ex-ADF staff are qualified at this level, compared to just 3% of Non-ADF staff. This likely accounts for much of the disparity in senior role membership between the groups. Broadly speaking, the majority of graduate and postgraduate qualifications recorded for staff can be associated with the technical skills identified in the previously discussed M&S taxonomy [3], with the addition of undergraduate arts degrees and postgraduate management qualifications.

Table 4. Proportion of Ex-ADF and Non-ADF staff with bachelors and masters qualifications

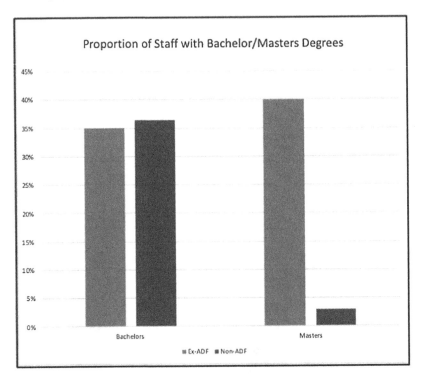

Lastly, in terms of educational background, vocational certificates and vendor certifications are also prevalent amongst CDAus simulation employees. In total, there are 154 vocational and vendor certificates recorded, at an average of 2.6 certificates per staff member. The distribution of certificates by employee ADF veteran status mimics that of other qualifications, with Ex-ADF employees averaging double the number of certificates (4 per person) when compared to non-ADF staff (2 per person).

At this juncture, it is relevant to consider the implications of these differences in qualification levels, and also the potential reasons why these differences occur. All levels of Cubic staff in 'Senior' roles have military backgrounds except in the constructive and federated simulation workforce, where it is only two in three. This significant difference is due to the fact that the technical skills required of this workforce are not resident in many of the trades and employment categories within the ADF. This may also go some way to explaining the differences in qualification levels. The dataset used in this case study does not include the age of employees, however, the lower number of years of experience for staff who are not ADF veterans is a likely indicator that this group of employees are younger in age. With this in mind, it is reasonable to assume that the combination of increased military experience and qualifications is a success factor for assuming senior roles. As a consequence, it would appear that technical skills and qualifications alone are not determinates of employee success.

Finally, we consider data collected by CDAus from historical exit records that provides reasons for separation (Table 5). Hours, career development and progression are primary reasons for 40% of departures and are outside the control of Cubic. Importantly, only 19% of the people who departed the organisation were Defence veterans, leaving a staggering 81% of departures accounted for by individuals without the tacit Defence knowledge that has been identified as key to success in these simulation roles. The data provided here does not allow for a full exploration of these issues (for example, if non-ADF employees more likely to cite lack of career opportunities as reasons for departure), and thus we identify this as an opportunity for future work.

Table 5. Historical workforce reasons given for separation (note % have been rounded and so total 101%)

Pay	Hours	Lack of career dev	Lack of career prog	Personal reasons	End of contract	Termination	Expectations not met	Other	Promotion
17%	10%	14%	16%	10%	6%	8%	5%	10%	5%

In summary, Cubic promotes based on a competitive process. In the context of this case study, staff with ADF backgrounds will have been provided with significant experience, training and education in leadership and management as part of their service roles. This results in those with prior Defence experience having an inherent advantage over those who do not when leadership roles arise. There are currently no formal pathways for obtaining 'leadership-in-simulation' qualifications, with internal mentoring and informal training the primary career development options. This unfortunately does not provide a formal mechanism for simulation professionals within CDAus to advance either within the organisation, or in a way that is recognised across sectors. Thus, staff retention emerges as a key challenge in sustaining and growing the simulation workforce, particularly as staff without in-depth domain knowledge appear more likely to leave and chase progression and leadership opportunities elsewhere. Thus the issue becomes self-reinforcing; if a subset of the staff are more likely to be retained within an organisation, then it should be apparent that those staff are also more likely to be promoted.

5   Discussion and Conclusion

A number of key issues affecting the simulation workforce were identified through this case study. Despite employing a higher proportion of staff that do not have a Defence background, Cubic employees at CDAus with this experience are more likely to be employed in senior roles. While the educational background of the employees supports this split in workforce (employees with higher level qualifications are appointed to senior roles), Cubic exit data points to systemic issues with staff retention and career progression. Ex-ADF personnel employed at Cubic represent 36% of the current and former workforce, but account for only 18% of departures. Thus, those without prior ADF service are significantly more likely to leave the organisation than ADF veterans. The critical importance of Defence experience to Cubic simulation roles, and particularly more senior roles, creates an effective career block for many workforce participants. A lack of relevant training or education pathways that provide equivalent or alternative career progression opportunities leave many employees with little option other than to seek advancement elsewhere. As well as increasing workforce costs, both in terms of time and money, issues with retaining simulation workforce only serve to compound the challenges associated with attracting appropriate personnel in the first instance.

The simulation position descriptions identified in the case study broadly align to existing frameworks and taxonomies associated with modelling and simulation roles. Employee qualifications stretch across vendor certification, vocational, graduate, and postgraduate programs, however, there is no clear transition or pipeline of qualification attainment that leads to senior simulation roles. Indeed, it has been suggested that "the majority of education and training offered in modeling and simulation lacks a firm pedagogical foundation" and that "employers are forced to adopt an ad hoc solution [...] by hiring students from a variety of specialty areas (e.g., various disciplines of engineering, computer science, aviation train-ing, and human factors) in the hope that capable students with these kinds of disciplinary backgrounds can be sufficiently well-trained on-the-job in the required M&S skills. While such job-oriented training may be the only option for employers, it is unlikely to be the optimum way to produce the M&S professionals needed to effectively develop and employ simulation targeted for education and training." [3, p. 277].

Our case study serves to illustrate these very issues. The bridge between the professional and technical skills required to perform in a simulation role, and the domain knowledge necessary to succeed in these roles, is difficult to traverse. Career progression emerges as a key source of workforce attrition. The lack of external, relevant training and educational pathways for employees places the burden for training with the employer. Adding to these challenges is the difficulty that employers face in finding appropriately qualified or suitably inclined employees in the first instance. Together, these issues present a challenge to the workforce that no doubt impacts on the ability to deliver current simulation capability, but more importantly, stymies innovation.

So, what is the solution? How do we create a modern simulation workforce that includes genuine and attractive career opportunities for people? The future development of the simulation workforce requires a holistic response from government, industry, and academia. While some efforts have been made, a universally accepted Simulation Body of Knowledge (SimBOK) continues to elude the profession [18, 19]. This may be due to highly integrated way that simulation is used within industries and sectors; it is difficult to generalise the technologies and skills of the profession when they are employed in very contextual ways. However, a BOK serves to define the set of concepts, terms, and activities that make up a professional domain, and thus outlines the core teachings and skills that are necessary for people looking to enter a profession.

Without this, a flow on effect to educational programs, role and position clarity, and professional development pathways occurs. In addition to establishing a common language for describing the simulation profession, two key strategies are required to advance and grow the capability of the simulation workforce. Firstly, educational programs across the full range of vocational and tertiary levels are required to establish entry and career development pathways for the simulation workforce. Secondly, a common set of simulation position descriptions, with consistent role expectations, will facilitate transfer of skills across simulation roles in different sectors, and also potentially from other role areas.

References

1. Okuda, Y., et al.: National growth in simulation training within emergency medicine residency programs, 2003–2008. Acad. Emerg. Med. **15**(11), 1113–1116 (2008). https://doi.org/10.1111/j.1553-2712.2008.00195.x
2. Kincaid, J.P., Hamilton, R., Tarr, R.W., Sangani, H.: Simulation in Education and Training. In: Obaidat, M.S., Papadimitriou, G.I. (eds.) Applied System Simulation, pp. 437–456. Springer, Boston (2003). https://doi.org/10.1007/978-1-4419-9218-5_19
3. Kincaid, J.P., Westerlund, J.P.: Simulation in education and training. In: Proceedings of the 2009 Winter Simulation Conference, Texas, 13–16 December (2009)
4. Galanis, G., Sottilare, R.: Fundamental Issues in Defense Training and Simulation. CRC Press, Boca Raton (2017)
5. Noetic Group: Navy, Army and Air Force simulation workforce study and design of a learning and development strategy. Internal Report: Unpublished (2017)
6. Cubic Corporation Homepage. https://cubic.com. Accessed 29 May 2019
7. Fishwick, P.A.: Computer simulation: growth through extension. Trans. Soc. Comput. Simul. **14**(1), 13–24 (1997). https://doi.org/10.1.1.50.8675
8. Hodson, D.D., Hill, R.R.: The art and science of live, virtual, and constructive simulation for test and analysis. J. Def. Model. Simul. **11**(2), 77–89 (2014)
9. Lenuik, T.A., et al.: Mixed Reality: The New Reality in DoD Decision Making. MODSIM World (2015)
10. Hodson, D.D.: Military simulation: a ubiquitous future. In: 2017 Winter Simulation Conference (WSC), pp. 4024–4025, December 2017. IEEE
11. Jenkins, Michael, Wollocko, Arthur, Negri, Alessandro, Ficthl, Ted: Augmented reality and mixed reality prototypes for enhanced mission command/battle management command and control (BMC2) execution. In: Chen, J.Y.C., Fragomeni, Gino (eds.) VAMR 2018. LNCS, vol. 10910, pp. 272–288. Springer, Cham (2018). https://doi.org/10.1007/978-3-319-91584-5_22
12. Kewley, R., Cook, J., Goerger, N., Henderson, D., Teague, E.: Federated simulations for systems of systems integration. In: Proceedings of the 40th Conference on Winter Simulation, pp. 1121–1129. Winter Simulation Conference, December 2008
13. Ryan, P., Clark, P., Ross, P., Fairleigh, M.: Interoperable aerospace training simulators within the australian defence force. In: SimTecT 2006 (2006)

14. Huiskamp, W., van den Berg, T.: Federated simulations. In: Setola, R., Rosato, V., Kyriakides, E., Rome, E. (eds.) Managing the Complexity of Critical Infrastructures. SSDC, vol. 90, pp. 109–137. Springer, Cham (2016). https://doi.org/10.1007/978-3-319-51043-9_6

15. Lee, E.A.: Cyber physical systems: design challenges. In: 2008 11th IEEE International Symposium on Object and Component-Oriented Real-Time Distributed Computing (ISORC), pp. 363–369. IEEE, May 2008

16. Dworschak, B., Zaiser, H.: Competences for cyber-physical systems in manufacturing–first findings and scenarios. Procedia CIRP 25, 345–350 (2014)

17. Szezerbicka, H., Banks, J., Rogers, R.V., Oren, T.I., Sarjoughian, H.S., Zeigler B.P.: Conceptions of curriculum for simulation education. In: Joines, J.A., Barton, R.R., Kang, K., Fishwick, P.A. (eds.) Proceedings of the 2000 Winter Simulation Conference, Piscataway, New Jersey, pp. 1635–1644. Institute of Electrical and Electronics Engineers, Inc. (2000)

18. Birta, L.G.: The quest for the modelling and simulation body of knowledge. In: Keynote presentation at the Sixth Conference on Computer Simulation and Industry Applications, Instituto Tecnologico de Tijuana, Mexico, 19–21 February 2003 (2003)

19. Ören, T.I.: Toward the body of knowledge of modeling and simulation. In: Interservice/Industry Training, Simulation, and Education Conference (I/ITSEC), pp. blank;1–19, December 2005

20. Jahangirian, M., et al.: Simulation in health-care: lessons from other sectors. Oper. Res. 12 (1), 45–55 (2012). https://doi.org/10.1007/s12351-010-0089-8

21. Quan, J., Cha, H.: IT certifications, outsourcing and information systems personnel turnover. Inf. Technol. People 23(4), 330–351 (2010). https://doi.org/10.1108/09593841011087798

22. Lo, J.: The information technology workforce: A review and assessment of voluntary turnover research. Inf. Syst. Front. 17(2), 387–411 (2015). https://doi.org/10.1007/s10796-013-9408-y

Machine Learning and Physiological Metrics Enhance Performance Assessment

Amy Dideriksen[1](✉) and Joseph Williams[2](✉)

[1] Collins Aerospace, 12600 Challenger Parkway, Suite 130,
Orlando, FL 32826, USA
Amy.Dideriksen@collins.com
[2] Collins Aerospace, 400 Collins Road NE, Cedar Rapids, IA 52498, USA
Joseph.Williams@collins.com

Abstract. Artificial Intelligence (AI) is the latest innovation being sought after by commercial and military training communities. Recent advances in big data collection and increased computer processing speed makes it possible to envision many beneficial applications in the modeling, simulation and training industry (Richbourg 2018).

Collecting and analyzing performance metrics in After Action Review (AAR) tools to personalize and adapt training is one application being researched. AAR tools collect, display and record performance metrics in real-time for providing feedback to the student upon completion of the exercise.

Understanding relevant data to collect and its appropriate use is still being proven through evidence-based research. Results from our research on measuring training effectiveness, enable us to assess the efficacy of training devices and content. Results demonstrate that assessment of training effectiveness must capture training readiness in terms of task performance with acceptable levels of cognitive workload.

Using the training effectiveness research data, we designed Deep Neural Networks to predict student performance. Results show that when cognitive workload is included as a feature in the DNN, it significantly increases the performance prediction to an extremely high level of accuracy. We developed data visualizations for instructors to review individual and class aggregate performance data. By integrating this methodology with AI technology, we have built the foundation for an intelligent AAR that can be applied to an adaptive learning solution.

Keywords: Artificial Intelligence · Big data · After Action Review · Personalize · Metrics · Feedback · Training effectiveness · Adaptive learning · Performance · Real-time · Physiological · Cognitive workload · Machine learning · Algorithm · Deep Neural Network · Predictive analytics · Data visualization

© Springer Nature Singapore Pte Ltd. 2019
A. Naweed et al. (Eds.): ASC 2019, CCIS 1067, pp. 129–138, 2019.
https://doi.org/10.1007/978-981-32-9582-7_10

1 Introduction

Artificial intelligence (AI) has been a disruptive technology. It is not an entirely new concept, as it began in the 1950's when a computer program was developed with the capability of defeating humans at a game of checkers (Samuel 2000). As AI has gone through a number of booms and busts, we are in the midst of our third boom and are seeing rapid growth in program development, strategic initiatives and continued investments from military and commercial industries (Richbourg 2018). Data analytics is becoming more prevalent with the growth in computer power. Machine learning methods such as deep learning have reached surprising performance levels in a variety of industries such as, social media, healthcare, finance, engineering, image and speech recognition (Woodard and Enloe 2018).

The training industry can also envision many benefits from applying machine learning techniques. For example, machine learning is currently being used in research to create synthetic images (Cheng et al. 2017) and synthetic characters (Ustun et al. 2018) and how behavior models can be used to automate decision-making assessments (Jensen and Ramachandran 2018). One of the most advantageous applications for the training industry is to use machine learning techniques in developing intelligent, after action review (AAR) tools. These tools can provide asynchronous learning, allowing students to complete training on their own time and at their own pace, without being dependent on a structured classroom environment or a human instructor for feedback. Implementing an objective performance assessment, integrated with machine learning techniques enables a real-time, personalized solution to each individual student.

There are several challenges in implementing successful artificial intelligent technologies, which are also applicable to the design and development of an intelligent AAR tool. Some of the biggest challenges are described below.

- **The right data**
  Many in the industry are designing intelligent solutions that focus on traditional assessment methods of evaluating task performance data. However, some programs, such as the Pilot Training Next program, are also beginning to include human system metrics along with task-performance metrics in their goal of reducing time to train through innovative technology solutions (Lewis and Livingston 2018). Knowing what data to collect is a difficult challenge.
- **Large data set**
  Having access to large amounts of data to train the machine learning algorithms is critical. Collecting task-specific performance data from training simulators and operational environments that is classified and labeled with Subject Matter input is difficult to capture. Physiological data collection has become easier with the influx of commercial-off-the-shelf wearable sensors.
- **Use of data**
  Knowing how to use the data to accomplish our goals is no simple task. Considerations need to be made regarding optimal use. For example, is there a requirement for the solution to be platform agnostic or designed to solve a very specific problem? Does the solution need to operate in real-time, or is post-processing acceptable?

This paper discusses one example of the "right" data, obtaining a ground-truth data set, and applications of how to use the data to accomplish the goal of developing an intelligent AAR tool.

2   The Right Data

Motivated by the continued investments made by the Government and commercial industries in simulation-based training, without having a valid method to measure training effectiveness, Collins Aerospace has invested in research to objectively measure training effectiveness. In collaboration with the University of Iowa Operator Performance Laboratory and the Faubert Applied Research Centre, we spent the last two years researching our methodology in measuring training effectiveness by assessing physiological measures in combination with task performance metrics (Hoke et al. 2017; Dideriksen et al. 2018).

One theory providing foundation for our research is the Cognitive Load Theory (Sweller 1988), which postulates that the accurate classification of the cognitive demands on the student during a training exercise may be one of the most important measures to assess the efficacy of a training device. Sweller's theory states that there are three sources of cognitive load that are competing for resources. The intrinsic load is related to task complexity, and are the resources required to understand the training materials. The germane load is associated with learning new material, and are the resources required for transferring learning to long-term memory. The extraneous load is associated with external cognitive demands and are the resources required to process information not related to the training.

For our study, physiological measures of cognitive workload were used to quantify total load through a Cognitive Assessment Tool Set (CATS) that captures and transforms electrocardiogram (ECG) waveforms into a quantitative signature of cognitive state. Real-time cognitive workload estimation is generated from ECG signals by the CATS software using a minimally intrusive system with body-worn electrodes and a biofeedback device. This system does not interfere with performance tasks. The ECG waveform is transformed from its scalar space to

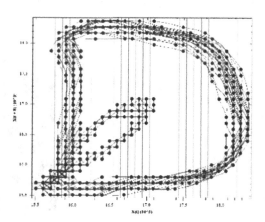

Fig. 1. Course grained representation

an embedded phase space, and then is coarse grained (Fig. 1) to provide a quantitative signature of cognitive state (Engler et al. 2013; Schnell and Engler 2014).

To measure spare cognitive capacity, we used a perceptual-cognitive measurement technique available through a commercial product known as NeuroTracker. Perceptual-cognitive skills refer to the role played by both perceptual and cognitive processes that are needed to extract meaningful information from a dynamic scene and support decision-making. NeuroTracker stimulates a high number of brain networks that must work together during the exercise including complex motion integration, dynamic, sustained and distributed attention processing and working memory (Faubert and Sidebottom 2012). The exercise requires attention and working memory as students track four targets among eight spheres following a linear trajectory projected within a cube space. NeuroTracker provided a secondary task used to quantify spare cognitive resources based on the displacement thresholds. Displacement thresholds represent how fast the balls are moving, where faster speeds are indicative of better performance (Fig. 2).

 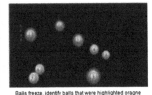

Track orange highlighted balls   Highlights disappear and balls begin to move   Balls freeze, identify balls that were highlighted oragne

Fig. 2. NeuroTracker task

In our past research, we assessed 30 aviation pilots performing various flight maneuvers in a simulator and with over 50 h in a live aircraft. Pilots were categorized into groups of 10 based on education and experience into three proficiency levels; novice, competent and expert.

The pilots performed flight maneuvers with a touchscreen display for NeuroTracker installed in the aft cockpit of a Velochody L-29 jet trainer. The L-29 is a dual-cockpit jet used as an "aircraft-in-the-loop" (AIL) simulator on the ground and as a live asset. The L-29 was equipped with the CATS software (OPL 2014) that collected flight technical and physiological data from the sensors and simulation system. The collected data was time-stamped, synchronized, and recorded to a database that supports data analysis.

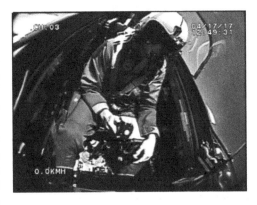

Fig. 3. Pilot in live flight

Each pilot performed easy, medium and hard flight maneuvers to assess their flight technical performance while using NeuroTracker as a secondary task to measure spare cognitive resources. Each participant also flew the three flight maneuvers without the perceptual-cognitive software present. The order of these scenarios was randomized for both the simulator and flight portions of the study. Figure 3 shows a pilot in live flight.

In addition to collecting objective metrics, pilots were asked to complete subjective, self-assessment surveys, including a 10-point Bedford workload scale.

2.1 Research Results

Overall, our research results help to validate our methodology and demonstrate that assessment of training effectiveness must capture training readiness in terms of levels of performance and appropriate levels of cognitive workload (Hoke et al. 2017; Dideriksen et al. 2018). The main takeaways from the results are listed below:

- **Perceptual-cognitive & physiological measures successfully differentiated between the simulator and live flight**
  Our research is consistent with previous research states that there is additional noise, and differing brain dynamics in real-world environments compared to lab environments (Hoke et al. 2017). Cognitive workload was higher for all pilots in the jet than the simulator.
- **Level of fidelity greatly effects experienced pilots more so than novice**
  Novice pilots scored higher on NeuroTracker tasks in the simulator than the jet, but pilots with more experience had reversed results. Competent and expert pilots had higher NeuroTracker scores in the jet than the simulator. They have a higher number of flight hours than novice pilots, and more deeply engrained expectation of a platforms flight dynamics. Since the simulator had a lesser degree of real flight dynamics, the more experienced pilots had to quickly adapt, requiring increased cognitive workload. The novice pilots did not have to adapt and had more spare cognitive capacity to spend concentrating on NeuroTracker. In flight, novice pilots were over-tasked in performing the maneuvers, and ignored the NeuroTracker task almost completely, and this was represented in their scores.
- **Experienced pilots are better able to multi-task**
  Competent and expert pilots outperformed novice pilots in the jet when Neuro-Tracker was absent, but worse when it was present. The more experienced pilots had a greater ability to share their attention between NeuroTracker and performing the flight maneuvers. Whereas the novice pilots "shed" performance on Neuro-Tracker tasks in live flight to focus their attention on navigating the aircraft.
- **Subjective assessments can be unreliable and invalid**
  On average, all pilots rated the simulator tasks as requiring higher cognitive load than the jet. This was not unexpected as simulator tasks were flown prior to the jet, and the more experienced pilots had to adapt to the differences from a live aircraft. All pilots under-rated their performance as it compared to their cognitive workload scores. This is a common concern with subjective assessments of workload as it is difficult to score your own performance.
- **Assessment of training effectiveness must include measures of performance and cognitive workload**
  Both NeuroTracker and flight maneuvers place cognitive workload demands on the pilot. If an assessment of the pilot's skill is evaluated with traditional methods, the

pilot may perform the task within specific task parameters in training, but if their cognitive workload is high it could lead to failure in an operational environment. And if the pilot were assessed based on cognitive workload alone, they may perform within an optimal workload range, but not within the task performance requirements.

In the context of this study, application of our methodology is recognized through the relationship of the student's physiological metrics and their flight technical performance. Figure 4 illustrates an example of cognitive workload (green line) mapped to a 10-point Bedford scale (right) and flight technical data (blue line) derived from a pilot in the 2017 study (Hoke et al.). The pilot was asked to perform a 360° turn holding a 30° angle of bank ($\pm2.5°$). Roll target and thresholds are highlighted in red horizontal lines.

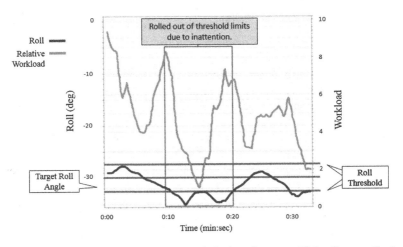

Fig. 4. Cognitive workload vs. flight technical performance (Color figure online)

Cognitive workload started high when the aircraft controls were given to the pilot. Cognitive workload dropped due to inattention, or lack of cognitive engagement, and the pilot exceeded the acceptable target range for the task. When the pilot realized the error and attempted to correct the maneuver to acceptable performance thresholds, cognitive workload spiked. Workload spiked a second time when the pilot realized he once again exceeded the threshold, and the error is corrected before giving the controls back to the safety pilot.

3   Large Data Set

Driven by the need to digitally enable our simulated training devices, we needed a large data set to train machine learning algorithms. Simple human-observation of the data would prove to be nearly impossible. We had access to large amounts of objective, recorded pilot cognitive state and flight technical data from our research. With 30 pilots flying multiple flight maneuvers in a simulator and live jet, and over 50+ h of live flight, we had approximately 1.2 million data points.

4 Use of Data

To accomplish our goal of enhancing our legacy AAR tool to allow instructors to monitor pilot task performance and cognitive workload in real-time, the next step in our process was to determine which features would be needed. We chose predictive analytics to support the foundation of an adaptive learning technology. As pilots perform training tasks, they accomplish the task at some degree of performance and expenditure of cognitive workload. As they perform multiple repetitions of this task, their performance improves, and cognitive workload expenditure decreases. An adaptive learning training system, using predictive analytics, could adjust the level of task difficulty during those task repetitions to maintain cognitive workload expenditure at an optimal level while performance rapidly continues to improve (Dideriksen et al. 2018). Our second feature was to develop data visualizations to assist instructors with individual and class aggregate performance results. Although this is a post-processing application, it is an important capability that can assist in identifying areas in need of improvement for both instructional content and student performance.

4.1 Predictive Analytics

We focused on developing a supervised learning algorithm using Deep Neural Networks to predict student performance (Dideriksen et al. 2019). Our goal was to demonstrate that pilot behavior is relatively predictable. We hypothesized that by including cognitive workload in combination with the analysis of flight technical metrics, it would increase the accuracy of our predictions.

We began by classifying the data, using data interpolation techniques to ensure that our data was being reviewed at the same data sample rate. Next we scored the pilots' flight technical performance for each flight maneuver. Grades were based on the last five seconds of flight time. This allows for a gradual change in grade. The grading system used is impossible for a pilot to get a perfect score, but was effective at representing changes in pilot performance.

4.2 Predictive Analytic Results

Results show that when cognitive workload is included in the neural network, it increases the performance prediction to an extremely high level of accuracy. Using preflight technical scores, the model was able to predict performance at 89% accuracy. Adding cognitive workload metrics consistently improved the accuracy of the machine learning models to 96%.

Figure 5 illustrates how the predicted score lines up with the actual performance score. In the top graph, the blue line represents the actual rolling grade from a low difficulty flight maneuver, and the yellow line represents the predicted grade, 20 s in the future, based on 5 s from the past. In the middle graph, the green line represents the pilot's performance deviation from the ideal for roll, and in the bottom graph, the red line represents the pilots performance deviation from the ideal for altitude.

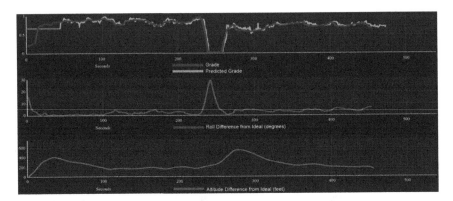

Fig. 5. Predictive performance analytics (Color figure online)

With the capability of predicting student performance in real-time, we can modify training content to maintain student engagement, which aids in the transfer and retention of requisite skills.

There are limitations to the neural networks in this study. The testing of all neural networks was based on historical data and has not yet been tested in real-time. To demonstrate that these machine learning models can actually predict future performance, live trials are needed. Using the neural networks to predict performance with adversarial subjects, such as pilots with no flight experience or motivation to succeed, may provide immensely different results.

4.3   Data Visualization

In order to visually display pilot performance from our research data, we developed a pipeline that has a sophisticated database, graphing, and data analytic tool set for visualizing complex data sets. We used high-level scripting languages to integrate multiple data analysis libraries quickly. These short, simple scripts can synthesize gigabytes of data, perform advanced data analytics, graph the data, and display graphical results reducing the information an instructor would need to process for overall performance assessment. Integrating machine learning into the data analytics pipeline lends to the application of many different neural network approaches for analysis and interpretation. The database, graphing, and analytics tools are mature and extendable, and can be specialized to address additional data challenges. This toolset combination creates a pipeline from raw data to human-understandable data metrics and analysis of results for fast prototyping and understanding.

The visual analytics displayed in Fig. 6 provides instructors with an insight into individual performance. This is an example of an individual pilot's performance flying a total of 22 flight maneuvers. The box in the upper left shows the pilot's first iteration of the maneuver. As you can see from the color scheme as it turns from purple to yellow, performance improved as the circle gets tighter, representing less deviation from the ideal flight pattern. The two graphs in the upper right are altitude and roll. The lower two graphs show cognitive workload and the rolling grade for performance. All of these charts are synchronized over time.

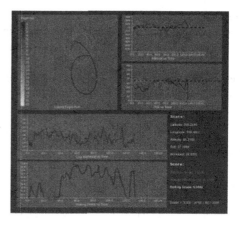

Fig. 6. Individual visualization (Color figure online)

Figure 7 shows the aggregate performance results of all 30 pilots. In the upper left is a Markov Model, which shows workload threshold transitions. This represents the predictability of pilots flying outside of the flight task parameters. The graph on upper right displays the number of occurrences over time within the threshold. The graph in the middle plots cognitive workload, and the lower two graphs show the average altitude and role versus time for all the pilots. The red lines in both illustrations represent the task parameters that pilots were to fly within.

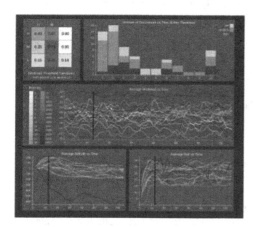

Fig. 7. Class visualization (Color figure online)

5 Conclusion

With the results from our research, we believe our training effectiveness methodology provides us with the right data. The large data set collected was used to develop machine learning algorithms to enhance performance assessment. Combining task performance and cognitive workload metrics in the predictive analytics models resulted in a high degree of accuracy. The benefit of being able to monitor and predict student performance in near real-time, enables personalized training to be implemented, ensure safety and maintain engagement through an optimal level of cognitive state. Data visualizations provide valuable insight to the instructor on individual and class performance data. Integrating both the predictive analytics and the data visualizations into an intelligent AAR for a simulated-training device can provide robust personalized training and is the foundation needed for an AI adaptive learning solution.

Acknowledgements. We would like to thank our research collaboration partners, Dr. Thomas Schnell from the University of Iowa Operator Performance Laboratory, and Jocelyn Faubert from the Faubert Applied Research Centre.

References

Cheng, Z., et al.: Human activity synthetic data generation. In: Interservice/Industry Training, Simulation, and Education Conference, Orlando, FL (2017)

Dideriksen, A., Williams, J., Avdic-McIntire, G.: The value of cognitive workload in machine learning predictive analytics (2019). Manuscript submitted for publication

Dideriksen, A., Reuter, C., Patry, T., Schnell, T., Hoke, J., Faubert, J.: Define "expert": characterizing proficiency for physiological measures of cognitive workload. In: Interservice/Industry Training, Simulation, and Education Conference, Orlando, FL (2018)

Engler, J., Schnell, T., Walwanis, M.: Deterministically nonlinear dynamical classification of cognitive workload. In: Interservice/Industry Training, Simulation, and Education Conference, Orlando, FL (2013)

Faubert, J., Sidebottom, L.: Perceptual-cognitive training of athletes. J. Clin. Sport. Psychol. **6**(1), 85–102 (2012)

Hoke, J., Reuter, C., Romeas, T., Montariol, M., Schnell, T., Faubert, J.: Perceptual-cognitive & physiological assessment of training effectiveness. In: Interservice/Industry Training, Simulation, and Education Conference, Orlando, FL (2017)

Jensen, R., Ramachandran, S.: Data-driven training development: deriving performance constraints from operational examples. In: Interservice/Industry Training, Simulation, and Education Conference, Orlando, FL (2018)

Lewis, J., Livingston, J.: Pilot training next: breaking institutional paradigms using student-centered multimodal learning. In: Interservice/Industry Training, Simulation, and Education Conference, Orlando, FL (2018)

OPL: Cognitive assessment tool set (CATS) user manual. Retrieved from Iowa City, Iowa (2014)

Richbourg, R.: Deep learning: measure twice, cut once. In: Interservice/Industry Training, Simulation, and Education Conference, Orlando, FL (2018)

Samuel, A.: Some studies in machine learning using the game of checkers. IBM J. Res. Dev. **44** (1.2), 206–226 (2000)

Schnell, T., Engler, J.: Entropic skill assessment of unmanned aerial systems (UAS) operators. J. Unmanned Veh. Syst. **2**(02), 53–68 (2014)

Sweller, J.: Cognitive load during problem solving: effects on learning. Cogn. Sci. **12**, 257–285 (1988)

Ustun, V., Rosenbloom, P., Sajjadi, S., Nuttall, J.: Controlling synthetic characters in simulations: a case for cognitive architectures and sigma. In: Interservice/Industry Training, Simulation, and Education Conference, Orlando, FL (2018)

Woodard, T., Enloe, M.: Deep learning applications for modeling, simulation, and training. In: Interservice/Industry Training, Simulation, and Education Conference, Orlando, FL (2018)

Author Index

Printed in the United States
By Bookmasters